M. T. Yates

First Lessons in Chinese

M. T. Yates

First Lessons in Chinese

ISBN/EAN: 9783337166311

Printed in Europe, USA, Canada, Australia, Japan

Cover: Foto ©Paul-Georg Meister /pixelio.de

More available books at **www.hansebooks.com**

法妙語譯西中

FIRST

LESSONS IN CHINESE.

BY

REV. M. T. YATES, D.D.

Revised and Corrected.

SHANGHAI:
AMERICAN PRESBYTERIAN MISSION PRESS.
1893.

AUTHOR'S INTRODUCTION.

THOSE who have attempted to acquire a working knowledge of any of the spoken dialects of China by picking up isolated words from a vocabulary or dictionary, (like picking pebbles from the sea shore), know full well the necessity of a beginner's book ; one that is practical, and yet so simple that the learner will be encouraged by being able to use his acquirements from the first lesson.

The design of the author of this manual is to supply, to some extent, this long-felt want ; and he is confident that any one who will take the trouble to master these lessons (the work of only a few months), will be in possession of the key to the spoken language, not only of this district, but, with a slight change in the sound of words (which can be easily acquired), of other districts also ; for the general structure of the language (barring a few localisms), is the same everywhere.

The importance of a thorough knowledge of the classifiers cannot be too strongly urged ; for it is impossible to speak of any visible object without using one of them, and it is important to a clear understanding of the matter under consideration that the correct classifier be used.

A careful study of the inflected verbs will save months, if not years, of perplexing uncertainty ; for the same forms will be found applicable to most other verbs.

PREFACE TO NEW EDITION.

ONLY a few books have been published for the purpose of aiding students in acquiring the Shanghai vernacular. Of these, none has been more helpful to beginners than that of Dr. Yates, which is now given to the public in a more convenient form, carefully revised and corrected, and with the old Romanization replaced by that of the present Union System. The ingenious but cumbersome phonetic representation of English sounds by Chinese characters has been omitted in this edition, and such corrections made as seemed necessary to bring the work into harmony with present usage; but the general plan of the book, and nearly all of the sentences, both Chinese and English, remain as before.

Mrs. Yates, believing that a new edition would be helpful to missionary students in preparing for their work, accepted the offer of the undersigned to prepare the work for the press. In this work many helpful suggestions have been received from Rev. G. F. Fitch, while two competent Chinese teachers, 鐘子能 and 屠仁鄉, have rendered valuable assistance in making corrections in the Chinese text.

J. A. SILSBY.

PRONUNCIATION OF SHANGHAI SYLLABLES AS REPRESENTED BY THE UNION SYSTEM OF ROMANIZATION.

THE true pronunciation of Chinese sounds can only be learned from a Chinese teacher. A large majority of the sounds have no true equivalent in English; hence the student should bear in mind that any *Romanization used does not represent English sounds, but Chinese sounds.* This fact can not be too strongly emphasized. The committee which formulated the present Union System of Romanization did not have in mind the representation of Chinese sounds by their nearest English equivalents so much as it had in view the production of a complete, simple and systematic table whereby all the Chinese sounds should be represented by Roman letters or combinations thereof,—and this without the use of diacritical marks. It should be borne in mind by the student that this system does not divide a word into all its phonetic elements; but rather does it follow a plan well-known to Chinese scholars; viz., that of dividing each syllable represented by a Chinese character into two elements,—one initial and one final.

THE INITIALS.

The Initials are divided into a "Higher," a "Middle" or "Aspirated," and a "Lower" Series.

1. The HIGHER SERIES comprises sounds represented by—*p, 'm, 'v, t, ts, s, 'l, 'n, 'ny, ng, k, ky, kw, pure vowel sounds, i* and *'w.*

2. The MIDDLE or ASPIRATED SERIES comprises sounds represented by—*p', f, t', ts', k', ch, k'w, h, hy* and *hw.*

3. The LOWER SERIES comprises sounds represented by—*b, m, v, d, dz, z, l, n, ny, ng, g, j, gw,* ʻ(*or low vowel sounds, slightly aspirated*), *y* and *w.*

N. B. Let it be remembered that the difference between the Higher and Lower Series of initial sounds *is not so much a difference in consonantal quality as a difference in pitch;* but there is a real consonantal difference.

The following descriptions of sounds may be found helpful, but the true sound in most cases must be learned from a Chinese teacher. After each description there is given a Chinese character representing, or containing, the sound described.

p—pronounced much the same as in English, but a little harder and without any aspiration. 百

p'—aspirated; somewhat as an American or Irishman would pronounce *p* in *pin*, but with a still more decided aspiration. 拍

b—not quite so hard as in English. 白

'*m*—higher and more explosive than *m*. 每

m—as in English. 煤

'*v*—a sound slightly harder and less aspirated than the English *f*. 勿

f—as in English. 法.

v—Nearly as in English, but often approaching *w*, with which it is often confused. 罰

t—harder and with less aspiration than in English. 丁

t'—softer and more aspirated. 聽

d—softer than in English. 停

ts—harder and less aspirated than in English. 節

ts'—softer and aspirated. 切

dz—softer than in English. The majority of Shanghai natives fail to distinguish between this sound and that represented by *z*. 集

s—as in English. 息

z—softer and more sibiliant than in English. 席

'*l*—higher and more explosive than '*l*. 拾

l—as in English. 鈴

'*n*—higher and more explosive than *n*. 乃

n—as in English. 內

'*ny*—higher and quicker than *ny*. 拈

ny—Much the same as *n* in *new*, but with a more decided *y* sound following the *n*. 年

'*ng*—higher and quicker than *ng*. 一 顔

ng—harder than *ng* in *song*. 顔

k—harder and with less aspiration than in English. 加

k‘—softer and with more aspiration. 揩

g—as in *go*, but softer. 茄

ky—a peculiar sound which can not be represented by any English combination. Perhaps *tky* might better represent it. 雞

ch—softer and with more aspiration than *ch* in *church*. 氣

j—a little harder than *j* in *jug*. 旗

kw—as *qu* in *quart*. 規

kw‘—the same sound aspirated and softer. 塊

gw—softer than *gu* in *Guelph*. 葵

Vowel initials are pronounced higher and purer than in English.

h—as in hat. 海, Confused with sounds by many natives.

'—before an initial vowel indicates that the word belongs to the lower series and that the vowel is slightly aspirated. This aspiration is little more than a huskiness in the throat attendant upon the lower pitch of the voice. It should not be confused with *h*. 害

i—lighter than the y sound,—as *i* in *view*. Only as an initial is the *y* sound given to *i*. In other positions *i* represents a vowel sound. 因

hy—somewhat like *sh* in *should*, but less sibilant. It is more like *ti* in *initial*. 興

y—as in *young*. 刑

'*w*—higher, lighter and quicker than *w*. 碗

hw—as *wh* in *where*. 歡

w—as in *way*. 完

DOK-YONG ZZ-MOO.

In this class there is no clear and distinct vowel sound. The final sound in the syllables *tsz*, *ts‘z*, *dz*, *sz* and *z* might be regarded as a vowel sound akin to that in the final syllable of *able*—prolonged, but without any *l* sound, as given by some foreigners. Edkins, Mateer, Baller and others represent this sound by *ï*, and would spell—*tsï, ts'ï, dzï, sï* and *zï*. Others insist that there is no true vowel sound in the syllables represented, and that there is only a prolonged sounding of *s* or *z*. The syllables represented by *m, r* and *ng*, have a slight vowel sound before the consonant, this sound being much the same as that represented by *ï* in the list just mentioned : *m* represents much the same sound as *m* in chasm—prolonged ; and *ng* is much the same as *ng* in song, but generally less sonant. *r* is an indescribable sound, between that of the English *r* and *l*,—or rather a blending of them. We give below a Chinese character representing the syllables described as *Dok-yong Zz-moo*.

| *m*—無 | *tsz*—此 | *sz*—思 | *r*—而 |
| *tsz*—紙 | *dzz*—池 | '*r*—耳 | *ng*—魚 |

THE FINALS.

The Finals are divided into three classes ; viz.,—

1. VOWEL ENDINGS, comprising sounds represented by—*a, e, i, au, o, oo, oe, eu, u, ui, ia, iau* and *ieu;* also the *Wên-li ie*.

2. NASAL ENDINGS, comprising sounds represented by—*ang, an, en, ien, ing, aung, ong, oen, ung, uin* and *iang*.

3. ABRUPT VOWEL ENDINGS, comprising sounds represented by—*ak, ah, eh, ih, auh, ok, oeh, uh* and *iak*.

The *ng* sounds are less distinct than the English *ng* in *song*.

Final *n* is sounded in the combination *uin*, but in other combinations does little more than lengthen out and impart a nasal quality to the preceding vowel.

Final *k* and *h* are not pronounced : they indicate that the preceding vowel is pronounced in a short, abrupt manner. Single vowels followed by *k* retain their original sound ;—followed by *h* are shortened.

The vowels are sounded as follows :—

a, ang, ak—*a* as in *father*. 挨 櫻 白
an, ah—*a* as in *mat*. 晏 押

e, en—*e* as in *prey*. 哀 暗

eh—*e* as in *met*. 末

i, ien—*i* as in *caprice*. 衣 先. In the combination *ien*, *ie* may be regarded as a diphthong, the *e* being lightly sounded, its quality being nearly that of *e* in *prey*.

ing, ih—*i* as in *pit*. 林 必

au, aung, auh—*au* as in *fraud*. 凹 方 惡

o—*o* as *o* in *no*. 馬

ong—*o* as *ou* in *mourn*, or as *oo* in *moon*. The true sound seems to lie between, or rather, it is a combination of the two English sounds in the words given. 翁

ok—*o* as in *mote*. 屋

oo—as in *moon*. 烏

oe, oen, oeh—*oe* somewhat as in the German Goethe. 歲 安 曷

eu—somewhat as *i* in *mirth*. *Eu* should be carefully distinguished from *ir* as in *sir*. Foreigners often mistake by adding an *r* to the vowel sound. 伛

ung, uh—*u* as in *sun*. 恩 德

u—somewhat as *oo* in *foot*, but lengthened out. 主

ui—as *u* in the French *vertu*. 雨

uin—*ui* somewhat like the preceding, but only to be learned from a Chinese teacher. 雲

ia, iang, iak—short *i* is followed by *a* as in *father*. 謝 雨 削

ieu—short *i* followed by *eu*. 洗

ie—an occasional sound used in reading *Wên-li*: short *i* is followed by a sound akin to *e* as in *prey*.

TONE SIGNS.

° to the left of a word indicates the tone to be °*zang-sung*.

° to the right indicates the *chui*°-*sung*.

Final *h* or *k* indicate the *zeh-sung*.

All other words are in the *bing-sung*.

INDEX.

	PAGE.		PAGE.
Abuse	143	Classifiers	4
Add to	144	Climb	148
Adjectives, comparison of	39	Come	90
Adverbs	46	Command	120
Anchor	137	Comfort	148
Arrange, manage	150	Conduct; to guide	132
Ascend	141	Confide to	144
Ascend; to get up	117	Confiscate	150
Ask; to enquire; to investigate	93	Congeal; to coagulate	146
Answer	149	Conjugation of verbs	69
Bake; to roast	114	Consecutive Conjunctions	51
Banish	150	Conjunctions, etc.	57
Be	78	Consider	150
Bear or press upon	141	Consult	147
Beckon	138	Contribute; to tax	131
Become rich	148	Cook	149
Beg	120	Counting	1
Begin; to commence	126	Count	134
Believe	110	Crawl	148
Betroth	145	Create a disturbance	149
Bind with a cord	121	Criticise	149
Bite; to bark	121	Cry	135
Blow	121	Curse	143
Boil	114	Cut a mortise	140
Boil (*as water*)	148	Cut (*with scissors*)	140
Bolt	148	Cut (*with a small knife*)	112
Bore	140	Cut (*with sword or large knife*)	112
Borrow or lend	131	Cut; to engrave	116
Break	123	Decapitate; to kill	113
Broil; grill	114	Deceive, mystify	151
Brush	118	Deceive; to defraud	141
Build	102	Demonstrative Pronouns	36
Build a wall	102	Defeat; to frustrate	149
Burn (*as fuel*)	148	Deny; to falsify one's word	144
Buy	96	Degrade	148
Calculate	144	Deport one's self; to treat	150
Call; to tell	140	Deposit with another	134
Cancel; to erase	149	Descend	142
Care for; be careful	146	Desire; to expect, to hope	142
Carry a load	126	Die	139
Carry in the arms (*as a child*)	138	Dig	119
Carve; to cut	140	Divide; to separate	146
Cast down	139	Do; to make	84
Cast; to found	146	Draw a carriage	145
Catch; to seize; arrest	117	Draw in or up by capstan	137
Change	139	Drive; to urge; to press	149
Change a dollar into cash	145	Dwell	120
Choose; to select	124	Dye	139

	PAGE.		PAGE.
Eat; to drink; to smoke, etc.	92	Kill	113
Economize	140	Kneel	150
Encroach upon (*as another's land*)	150	Know	103
Envy	141	Laugh	136
Examine; to scrutinize	147	Lead (*as an animal*)	132
Exchange; to barter	145	Lean against	143
Exercises with verbs	83	Learn	122
Fail in business	146	Let go; to put down	127
Fall	123	Light a fire	116
Fall sick	145	Light a lamp	116
Fall (*as the tide*)	124	Line; to score	143
Fall down (*as a house*)	137	Listen	108
Fear; to dread	118	Live	139
File (*with a file*)	149	Lock; a lock	148
Feel	147	Look; to see	105
Finished	151	Look for	107
Flee; run away	125	Lose	136
Float	146	Lose	132
Fly	125	Lose (*in trade*)	148
Follow	146	Lower or take in sail	137
Forbid; to prohibit	150	Loot	141
Forfeit	150	Make ashamed	140
Forget	106	Make a record; to ascend	141
Forsake; to desert	125	Make a prostration	150
Freeze	146	Manage; to have the management of	147
Gamble	141	Measure	140
Gain (*profit*)	148	Meet together	139
Gather (*as fruit or flowers*)	149	Meet; to come in contact with	133
Gender of nouns	42	Melt; to dissolve	146
Give birth to; to rear	120	Mix; to get things confused	141
Give; hand; to give in marriage	99	Mood	65
Go	88	Move	119
Graft; to splice	142	Nail	139
Grind; to whet	149	Nod	145
Guard; to be careful	146	Number and person of verbs	68
Guess	147	Numerals	1
Hand or deliver in person	133	Nurse (*the sick*)	148
Hang or suspend	125	Offend; to transgress	150
Haul (*as on a rope*)	137	Open; to commence	128
Have	84	Pawn	145
Heal	148	Pay a balance	149
Hide or conceal	128	Pay money	100
Hide or secrete one's self	150	Personal Pronouns	27
Hinder	149	Peek (*as a fowl*)	143
Hoist a sail	137	Persuade	145
Hook	151	Perspire	135
Hours, days of the week, months, etc.	61	Pile one on top of another	144
Hypothecate	145	Plane	140
Imitate; to follow the example, etc.	146	Plant	119
Indefinite Pronouns	38	Play (*as an instrument*)	147
Inform	135	Plaster (*as a wall*)	149
Injure	148	Plural of Nouns	43
Institute a suit at law	135	Point with the hand	150
Interpret	147	Pound (*in a mortar*)	149
Interrogative Pronouns	31	Pour out	144
Interrogatives	59	Pray	146
Invite	143	Prepositions	53
Iron; to burn or scald	116	Present	139
Jump; to leap	148	Press down; to oppress	138
Kick	136	Print	136

	PAGE.		PAGE.
Prop	146	Sleep	144
Prove; to evince	147	Smell	145
Provide	118	Soak; to immerse, to baptize	148
Pry (*with a lever*)	140	Solder	146
Punish	147	Speak; to affirm or testify	94
Push; to shove	137	Spill	135
Put down a sedan	139	Spin	135
Put; to place	131	Splash	148
Quarrel	143 and 146	Split	112
Rap, knock	112	Sport; to frolic; to trifle	147
Read	133	Spread	135
Rebel	150	Spread; to propagate	148
Receive; to collect	101	Spread, daub or smear	150
Receive or accept	133	Squeeze	138
Recognize; to confess	142	Stab	143
Recommend	149	Stand	103
Reconcile; pacify	149	Steal	135
Reduce; to take from	147	Step upon	137
Regret	146	Stick; to adhere	124
Regretted	143	Stick (*in the ground, as a flag, etc.*)	139
Reject	147	Stir; to agitate	145
Repair	127	Stop	138
Repeat from memory	143	Strain; to filter	149
Repent	146	Strike; to chastise	110
Rely upon	144	String (*as cash*)	148
Remember	143	Strive	135
Retain; to detain	143	Stultify	150
Return what has been borrowed	136	Swear	135
Ride on horse-back	117	Sweep	113
Ring a bell	144	Swim	135
Rise (*as tide, etc.*)	123	Take	116
Roll	148	Take by force	141
Roll up	135	Take from	144
Rot or decay	134	Take hold of	127
Row a boat	144	Take up with both hands	150
Run	134	Take to pieces, or down	138
Run (*as water*)	147	Take the anchor	137
Sacrifice to	151	Tear	135
Save (*life or property*)	146	Tempt	142
Save (*time or labor*)	140	Tense	66
Saw	113	Think; to consider	109
Scrape	142	Throw away	139
Scratch	140	Throw (*as a stone*)	124
Seal; to deify; to exalt	140	Tie	142
Secure; to become security for	145	Tie (*as a parcel*)	121
Seize	138	Tow or track (*as a boat*)	137
Sell	98	Transfer	145
Sell on credit	143	Translate	147
Send forth; to issue	149	Turn (*as a wheel*)	146
Separate; to make distinct	149	Turn over	147
Sew, stitch	115	Turn round	147
Sift	149	Twist; to wring	138
Shave	134	Twist (*with the fingers*)	138
Shut; to close	129	Uncover; to open	150
Sing	135	Understand	104
Sink	135	Vacillate, to disappoint	150
Sit	102	Varnish or paint	140
Sit or stay with for company	148	Verbs, and inflection of the verb *to eat*	65
Skin; peel; strip	147	Verb *to be*	78
Slander	148	Violate a law or regulation	149

		PAGE.			PAGE.
Wait	... ...	138	Welcome a visitor	... ...	139
Walk	... ...	134	Wet	... ...	142
Water (*as a garden*)	... ...	149	Win	... ...	136
Waste, to squander	... ...	140	Wipe	... ...	115
Wash	... ...	114	Worship	... ...	138
Wear	... ...	135	Wrangle	... ...	143
Weave	... ...	135	Write	... ...	113
Weigh	... ...	140	Yield; to give place to	... ...	147
Weights, etc.	... ...	60			

FIRST LESSONS IN CHINESE.

NUMERALS.

1. One.	I.	一	*ih.*
2. Two.	II.	二	*nyi°.*
3. Three.	III.	三	*san.*
4. Four.	IV.	四	*sz°.*
5. Five.	V.	五	*°ng.*
6. Six.	VI.	六	*lok.*
7. Seven.	VII.	七	*ts'ih.*
8. Eight.	VIII.	八	*pah.*
9. Nine.	IX.	九	*°kyeu.*
10. Ten.	X.	十	*zeh.*
11. Eleven.	XI.	十一	*zeh-ih.*
12. Twelve.	XII.	十二	*zeh-nyi°.*
13. Thirteen.	XIII.	十三	*zeh-san.*
14. Fourteen.	XIV.	十四	*zeh-sz°.*
15. Fifteen.	XV.	十五	*°so-ng.*
16. Sixteen.	XVI.	十六	*zeh-lok.*
17. Seventeen.	XVII.	十七	*zeh-ts'ih.*
18. Eighteen.	XVIII.	十八	*zeh-pah.*
19. Nineteen.	XIX.	十九	*zeh-°kyeu.*
20. Twenty.	XX.	念	*nyan°.*

21.	Twenty-one. XXI.	廿一	nyan°-ih.
22.	Twenty-two. XXII.	廿二	nyan-nyi°.
23.	Twenty-three. XXIII.	廿三	nyan°-san.
24.	Twenty-four. XXIV.	廿四	nyan-sz.°
25.	Twenty-five. XXV.	廿五	nyan°-ng.
26.	Twenty-six. XXVI.	廿六	nyan°-lok.
27.	Twenty-seven. XXVII.	廿七	nyan°-ts'ih.
28.	Twenty-eight. XXVIII.	廿八	nyan°-pah.
29.	Twenty-nine. XXIX.	廿九	nyan°-°kyeu.
30.	Thirty. XXX.	三十	san-seh.
40.	Forty. XL.	四十	sz°-seh.
50.	Fifty. L.	五十	°ng-seh.
60.	Sixty. LX.	六十	lok-seh.
70.	Seventy. LXX.	七十	ts'ih-seh.
80.	Eighty. LXXX.	八十	pah-seh.
90.	Ninety. XC.	九十	°kyeu-seh.
100.	One hundred. C.	一百	ih pak.
101.	One hundred and one. CI.	一百零一	ih pak ling ih.
102.	One hundred and two. CII.	一百零二	ih pak ling nyi°.
103.	One hundred and three. CIII.	一百零三	ih pak ling san.
104.	One hundred and four. CIV.	一百零四	ih pak ling sz°.
105.	One hundred and five. CV.	一百零五	ih pak ling °ng.
106.	One hundred and six. CVI.	一百零六	ih pak ling lok.
107.	One hundred and seven. CVII.	一百零七	ih pak ling ts'ih.
108.	One hundred and eight. CVIII.	一百零八	ih pak ling pah.
109.	One hundred and nine. CIX.	一百零九	ih pak ling °kyeu.
110.	One hundred and ten. CX.	一百十	ih pak zeh.

111.	One hundred and eleven. CXI	一百十一	*ih pak zeh-ih.*
200.	Two hundred. CC.	二百	*nyi° pak.*
300.	Three hundred. CCC.	三百	*san pak.*
400.	Four hundred. CCCC.	四百	*sz° pak.*
500.	Five hundred. D.	五百	*°ng pak.*
600.	Six hundred. DC.	六百	*lok pak.*
700.	Seven hundred. DCC.	七百	*ts'ih pak.*
800.	Eight hundred. DCCC.	八百	*pah pak.*
900.	Nine hundred. DCCCC.	九百	*°kyeu pak.*
1000.	One thousand. M.	一千	*ih ts'ien*
1001.	One thousand and one.	一千零零一	*ih ts'ien ling ling ih.*
2000.	Two thousand.	二千	*nyi° ts'ien.*
5000.	Five thousand.	五千	*°ng ts'ien.*
10,000.	Ten thousand.	一萬	*ih man°.*
20,000.	Twenty thousand.	二萬	*nyi° man.*
50,000.	Fifty thousand.	五萬	*°ng man°.*
100,000.	One hundred thousand.	十萬	*zeh man°.*
500,000.	Five hundred thousand.	五十萬	*°ng-seh man°.*
900,000.	Nine hundred thousand.	九十萬	*°kyeu-seh man°.*
1,000,000.	One million.	一百萬	*ih pak man°.*

CLASSIFIERS.

In spoken Chinese, the force of the articles "a" or "an" is expressed by the numeral 一 (ih). All nouns take a word between the article and the noun, which may be denominated a *classifier*, as each of these different words denotes a class of objects. It is highly desirable that every student of the spoken language should, at the commencement of his studies, become thoroughly acquainted with these classifiers and the class of objects denoted by each; for a correct use of the classifiers will greatly facilitate communication with the Chinese. If a correct classifier be used before a word, it often leads to the meaning of that word, even if it be incorrectly pronounced. It must be borne in mind, however, that in Chinese, as well as in other languages, there are exceptions to all rules. A few nouns take two different classifiers.

First Classifier 个 (*kuh*).

A man.	一个人	*ih kuh nyung.*
A woman.	一个女人	*ih kuh °nyui-nyung.*
An unmarried woman.	一个小姐	*ih kuh °siau-tsia.*
A son.	一个兒子	*ih kuh °'eu-°tsz,* or *ih kuh nyi-°tsz.*
A daughter.	一个囡	*ih kuh noen.°*
A friend.	一个朋友	*ih kuh bang-yeu.*
A mandarin.	一个官府 or 一个官	*ih kuh kwen-°foo,* or *ih kuh kwen.*
A soldier.	一个兵丁 or 一个兵	*ih kuh ping-ting,* or *ih kuh ping.*
A native.	一个本地人	*ih kuh °pung-di-nyung.*
A servant.	一个用人	*ih kuh yong°-nyung.*

A sedan cooly.	一个轎班 or 一个轎夫	ih kuh jau°-pan, or ih kuh jau°-foo.
A sun.	一个日頭	ih kuh nyih-deu.
A moon.	一个月	ih kuh nyoeh.
A star.	一个星	ih kuh sing.
A body.	一个身體	ih kuh sung-°t'i.
A head.	一个頭	ih kuh deu.
A face.	一个面孔	ih kuh mien°-k'ong.
A heart.	一个心	ih kuh sing.
A nose.	一个鼻頭	ih kuh bih-deu.
A doorway.	一个門口	ih kuh mung-°k'eu.
A cannon.	一个砲	ih kuh p'au°.
A battery.	一个砲臺	ih kuh p'au°-de.
A bottle.	一个玻璃瓶	ih kuh poo-li-bing.
A hat, cap, or bonnet.	一个帽子	ih kuh mau°-°tsz.
A stove.	一个火爐	ih kuh °hoo-loo.
A grate.	一个火炕	ih kuh °hoo-k'aung°.
A dollar.	一个洋錢	ih kuh yang-dien.
A cash.	一个銅錢	ih kuh dong-dien.
A loaf.	一个饅頭	ih kuh men-deu.
A cake.	一个鷄蛋糕	ih kuh kyi-dan-kau.
A biscuit.	一个餶餅	ih kuh t'ah-°ping.
A buddhist priest.	一个和尙	ih kuh 'oo-zaung°.
A nun.	一个尼姑	ih kuh nyi-koo.
A tauist priest.	一个道士	ih kuh dau°-z.
A grave mound.	一个墳山	ih kuh vung-san.
An egg.	一个蛋	ih kuh dan°.

A scholar.	一个讀書人	*ih kuh dok-su-nyung.*
A merchant.	一个生意人	*ih kuh sang-i°-nyung.*
A farmer.	一个種田人	*ih kuh tsong°-dien-nyung.*
A carpenter.	一个木匠	*ih kuh mol-ziang°.*
A mason.	一个泥水匠	*ih kuh nyi-°sz-ziang°.*
A painter.	一个漆匠	*ih kuh t'sih-ziang°.*
A tailor.	一个裁縫	*ih kuh ze-vong.*
A stone mason.	一个石匠	*ih kuh zak-ziang°.*
A horse boy.	一个馬夫	*ih kuh °mo-foo.*
A table boy.	一个細者	*ih kuh si-tse°.*

SECOND CLASSIFIER, 隻 (*tsak*), DENOTES ALL ANIMALS, FOWLS, BIRDS, AND INSECTS; ALSO ALL ARTICLES OF FURNITURE HAVING FEET OR LEGS, OR RESTING ON A BASE; ALSO VESSELS, BOATS, ETC.

An elephant.	一隻象	*ih tsak °ziang.*
A camel.	一隻駱駝	*ih tsak lauh-doo.*
A lion.	一隻獅子	*ih tsak sz-°tsz.*
A tiger.	一隻老虎	*ih tsak °lau-°hoo.*
A cow.	一隻牛	*ih tsak nyeu.*
A water buffalo.	一隻水牛	*ih tsak °sz-nyeu.*
A deer.	一隻鹿	*ih tsak lok.*
A sheep.	一隻羊	*ih tsak yang.*
A goat.	一隻山羊	*ih tsak san-yang.*
A hog.	一隻猪玀	*ih tsak tsz-loo.*
A dog.	一隻狗	*ih tsak °keu.*

A cat.	一隻猫	ih tsak mau.
A wild cat.	一隻野猫	ih tsak °ya-mau.
A rat.	一隻老鼠 or 一隻老䑕	ih tsak °lau-°t'sz (°sz, °su,) or ih tsak °lau-dzong.
A hare.	一隻兔子	ih tsak t'oo°-°tsz.
A mule.	一隻騾子	ih tsak loo-°tsz.
A donkey.	一隻驢子	ih tsak li-°tsz.
A fox.	一隻狐狸	ih tsak 'oo-li.
A wolf.	一隻豺狼	ih tsak za-laung.
A squirrel.	一隻松鼠	ih tsak song-°su.
A weasel.	一隻黄狼	ih tsak waung-laung.
A fowl.	一隻鷄	ih tsak kyi.
A pheasant.	一隻野鷄	ih tsak °ya-kyi.
A duck.	一隻鴨	ih tsak ah.
A goose.	一隻鵝	ih tsak ngoo.
A turkey.	一隻火鷄	ih tsak °hoo-kyi.
A bird.	一隻鳥	ih tsak °tiau.
A snipe.	一隻竹鷄	ih tsak tsok-kyi.
A quail.	一隻鵪鶉	ih tsak en-dzung.
A crow.	一隻老鴉	ih tsak °lau-au.
A magpie.	一隻鴉雀	ih tsak au-ts'iak.
A hawk.	一隻鷹	ih tsak iung.
A minor.	一隻百哥	ih tsak pak-koo or pak-kwung.
A sparrow.	一隻廊雀	ih tsak mo-ts'iak, or mo-tsiang.
A swallow.	一隻燕子	ih tsak ien°-°tsz.

A pigeon.	一隻鴿子	*ih tsak keh-°tsz.*
A dove.	一隻孛鴣	*ih tsak beh-koo.*
A crab.	一隻蟹	*ih tsak °ha.*
A butterfly.	一隻蝴蝶	*ih tsak 'oo-dih.*
A bee.	一隻蜜蜂	*ih tsak* (or 一个) *mih-fong.*
A mosquito.	一隻蚊子	*ih tsak* (or 一个) *mung-°tsz.*
A wasp.	一隻胡蜂	*ih tsak* (or 一个) *'oo-fong.*
A table.	一隻檯子	*ih tsak de-°tsz.*
A chair.	一隻椅子	*ih tsak iui°-°tsz.*
A stool.	一隻杌子	*ih tsak ngeh-°tsz.*
A chest of drawers.	一隻抽檯	*ih tsak ts'eu-de.*
A drawer.	一隻抽屜	*ih tsak ts'eu-t'i.*
A trunk or box.	一隻箱子	*ih tsak siang-°tsz.*
A small box.	一隻匣子	*ih tsak °ah-°tsz.*
A bed.	一隻床	*ih tsak zaung.*
A couch.	一隻彌陀榻	*ih tsak mi-doo-t'ah.*
A washstand.	一隻揩面檯子	*ih tsak k'a mien de-°tsz.*
A dining table.	一隻吃飯檯子	*ih tsak chuh van de-°tsz.*
An office desk.	一隻寫字檯	*ih tsak °sia-z°-de.*
A bucket, tub, or cask.	一隻桶	*ih tsak °dong.*
A water kong.	一隻水缸	*ih tsak sz°-kaung.*
A shoe of sycee.	一隻元寶	*ih tsak nyoen-°pau.*
A hand.	一隻手	*ih tsak °seu.*
A foot and lower leg.	一隻脚	*ih tsak kyak.*
A finger.	一隻指頭	*ih tsak tsih-deu.*

An ear.	一隻耳朶	*ih tsak °nyi-°too.*
A wash bowl.	一隻面盆	*ih tsak mien°-bung.*
A plate.	一隻盆子	*ih tsak bung-°tsz.*
A dish.	一隻長盆子	*ih tsak dzang bung-°tsz.*
A saucer.	一隻茶盆子	*ih tsak dzo bung-°tsz.*
A cup.	一隻杯子	*ih tsak pe-°tsz.*
A glass.	一隻玻璃杯子	*ih tsak poo-li pe-°tsz, ih tsak poo-li pe.*
A wine glass.	一隻酒杯	*ih tsak °tsieu pe.*
A cooking stove.	一隻鉄灶	*ih tsak t'ih-tsau°.*
A clock.	一隻自鳴鐘	*ih tsak z°-ming-tsong.*
A watch.	一隻表	*ih tsak piau.*
A well.	一隻井	*ih tsak °tsing.*
A basket.	一隻籃	*ih tsak lan.*
A vessel or boat.	一隻船	*ih tsak zen.*
A nail.	一隻釘	*ih tsak ting.*
An apple.	一隻花紅	*ih tsak hwo-°ong.*
An orange.	一隻橘子	*ih tsak kyoeh-°tsz.*
A peach.	一隻桃子	*ih tsak dau-°tsz.*
A pear.	一隻生梨	*ih tsak sang-li.*
One (of this class.)	一隻	*ih tsak.*

THIRD CLASSIFIER, 把 (*°po*), DENOTES TOOLS, INSTRUMENTS OR ARTICLES USED IN THE HAND, TOOLS, ETC.

A knife or sword.	一把刀	*ih °po tau.*
A fork.	一把叉	*ih °po ts'o.*

A spoon.	一把抄	ih °po ts'au.
A hammer.	一把榔頭	ih °po laung-deu.
A file.	一把銼刀	ih °po ts'oo°-tau.
An ax.	一把斧頭	ih °po °foo-deu.
A saw.	一把鋸子	ih °po ke°-°tsz.
A chisel.	一把鑿子	ih °po zauh-°tsz.
A pair of scissors.	一把剪刀	ih °po °tsien-tau.
A pair of tongs.	一把火鉗	ih °po °hoo-jien.
A chair.	一把椅子	ih °po iui°-°tsz.
A fan.	一把扇子	ih °po sen°-°tsz.
A lock.	一把鎖	ih °po °soo.
A key.	一把鑰匙	ih °po yak-dz.
A broom.	一把掃帚	ih °po °sau-°tseu.
A tea pot.	一把茶壺	ih °po dzo-'oo.
A kettle.	一把鉛壺	ih °po k'an-'oo.
An umbrella.	一把傘	ih °po san°.
One (or a handfull)	一把	ih °po.

Fourth Classifier, 條 (*diau*), denotes objects long and winding or limber.

A river or large stream.	一條江	ih diau kaung.
A river or large stream.	一條河	ih diau 'oo.
A creek or canal.	一條浜	ih diau pang.
A ditch.	一條溝	ih diau keu.
A covered sewer.	一條陰溝	ih diau iung-keu.

An open sewer or drain.	一條陽溝	*ih diau yang-keu.*
A bridge.	一條橋	*ih diau jau.*
A road.	一條路	*ih diau loo°.*
A street.	一條街	*ih diau ka.*
An alley.	一條衖堂	*ih diau long°-daung.*
A rope.	一條繩	*ih diau zung.*
A tape or ribbon.	一條帶	*ih diau ta°.*
A strip of matting.	一條席	*ih diau zih.*
A quilt or blanket.	一條被頭	*ih diau °bi-deu.*
A mattress.	一條褥子	*ih diau nyok-°tsz.*
A sheet.	一條單被	*ih diau tan-°bi.*
A carpet.	一條毛單	*ih diau mau-tan.*
A pair of trowsers.	一條袴子	*ih diau k'oo°-°tsz.*
A handkerchief.	一條絹頭	*ih diau kyoen°-deu.*
A towel.	一條手巾	*ih diau °seu-kyung.*
A dragon.	一條龍	*ih diau long.*
A fish.	一條魚	*ih diau ng.*
A snake.	一條蛇	*ih diau zo.*
An eel.	一條鱔鯉	*ih diau men-li.*
A bar of iron.	一條鉄條	*ih diau t'ih-diau.*
A gold bar.	一條金條	*ih diau kyung-diau.*
One's life.	一條性命	*ih diau sing°-ming°.*
One (of this class).	一條	*ih diau.*

FIFTH CLASSIFIER, 根 (*kung*), DENOTES OBJECTS LONG AND USUALLY STIFF.

A stick of timber.	一根木頭	*ih kung mok-deu.*
A bamboo.	一根竹頭	*ih kung tsok-deu.*

A rattan.	一根籐	*ih kung dung.*
A cane or stick.	一根棒	*ih kung °baung.*
A boat's mast.	一根檣子	*ih kung ziang-°tsz.*
A straw.	一根草	*ih kung °ts'au.*
A stem or stalk (of plants).	一根梗	*ih kung °kang.*
A rope.	一根繩	*ih kung zung.*
A thread.	一根線	*ih kung sien°.*

SIXTH CLASSIFIER, 本 (°*pung*), DENOTES BOOKS, VOLUMES.

A volume, a book.	一本書	*ih °pung su.*
An account book.	一本帳簿	*ih °pung tsang°-°boo.*
A small blank book.	一本簿子	*ih °pung °boo-°tsz.*

SEVENTH CLASSIFIER, 部 (°*boo*), DENOTES AN ENTIRE WORK OF ONE OR MORE VOLUMES.

A work of one or more volumes.	一部書	*ih °boo su.*

EIGHTH CLASSIFIER, 座 (*zoo*°), DENOTES MASSIVE OBJECTS.

A mountain.	一座山	*ih zoo° san.*
A city.	一座城	*ih zoo° dzung.*
A temple.	一座廟	*ih zoo° miau°.*
A house.	一座房子	*ih zoo° vaung-°tsz.*

A two-storey house.	一座樓	ih zoo° leu.
A pagoda.	一座塔	ih zoo° t'ah.
One (of this class).	一座	ih zoo°.

NINTH CLASSIFIER, 疋 (p'ih), DENOTES WHOLE PIECES OF GOODS.

A piece of cloth.	一疋布	ih p'ih poo°.
A piece of broad cloth.	一疋哆囉呢	ih p'ih too-loo-nyi.
A piece of silk.	一疋綢	ih p'ih dzeu.
A piece of satin.	一疋緞子	ih p'ih doen°-°tsz.
A piece of velvet.	一疋絨	ih p'ih nyong.
A piece of shirting.	一疋洋布	ih p'ih yang-poo°.
A piece of drilling.	一疋斜紋布	ih p'ih zia-vung-poo°.
A piece of camlet.	一疋羽毛	ih p'ih °yui-mau.
A piece of grass cloth.	一疋麻布	ih p'ih mo-poo°.
A piece of white shirting.	一疋漂白布	ih p'ih p'iau bak poo°.
A piece of long ells.	一疋哔𠲿	ih p'ih pih-kyi.

ELEVENTH CLASSIFIER, 匹 (p'ih), DENOTES HORSES.

A horse.	一匹馬	ih p'ih °mo.
A mule.	一匹騾子	ih p'ih loo-°tsz.

TWELFTH CLASSIFIER, 塊 (kw'e°), DENOTES SLICES OR PORTIONS OF THINGS.

A piece of wood.	一塊木頭	ih kw'e° mok-deu.
A slab, a piece of stone.	一塊石頭	ih kw'e° zak-deu.

A board.	一塊板	*ih kw'e° °pan.*
A slice of meat.	一塊肉	*ih kw'e° nyok.*
A slice of bread.	一塊饅頭	*ih kw'e° men-deu.*
A piece of land.	一塊地皮	*ih kw'e° di°-bi.*
A pane of glass.	一塊玻璃	*ih kw'e° poo-li.*
A dollar.	一塊洋錢	*ih kw'e° yang-dien.*
A brick.	一塊砳磚	*ih kw'e° lok-tsen.*
A bit of cloth.	一塊布	*ih kw'e° poo°.*
A bit of silver, etc.	一塊銀子	*ih kw'e° nyung-°tsz.*

THIRTEENTH CLASSIFIER, 幅 (*fok*), DENOTES PAINTINGS OR ENGRAVINGS, ETC.

A painting or engraving.	一幅畫	*ih fok wo°.*
A chart or map.	一幅地理圖	*ih fok di°-°li-doo.*

FOURTEENTH CLASSIFIER, 扇 (*sen°*), DENOTES BROAD OBJECTS.

A door.	一扇門	*ih sen° mung.*
A window.	一扇窗	*ih sen° ts'aung.*
A screen.	一扇屏風	*ih sen° bing-fong.*
A fixed screen.	一扇屏門	*ih sen° bing-mung.*
A sail.	一扇篷	*ih sen° bong.*

FIFTEENTH CLASSIFIER, 乘 (*dzung*), DENOTES MACHINERY.

A steam engine.	一乘火輪機器	*ih dzung °hoo-lung kyi-chi°.*

A mill.	一乘磨子	*ih dzung moo°-°tsz.*
A loom.	一乘布機	*ih dzung poo°-kyi.*
A carriage.	一乘馬車	*ih dzung °mo-ts'o.*
A rail road carriage.	一乘火輪車子	*ih dzung °hoo-lung ts'o-°tsz.*
A flight of stairs, or a ladder.	一乘扶梯	*ih dzung voo-t'i (or woo-t'i).*
A step of a door.	一乘踏步	*ih dzung dah-boo°.*
An irrigating machine.	一乘水車	*ih dzung °sz-ts'o.*

SIXTEENTH CLASSIFIER, 頂 (°ting).

A sedan chair.	一頂轎子	*ih °ting jau°-°tsz.*
A hat.	一頂帽子	*ih °ting mau°-°tsz.*
An umbrella.	一頂傘	*ih °ting san°.*

SEVENTEENTH CLASSIFIER, 位 (we°), A TERM OF RESPECT.

A visitor, a customer.	一位客人	*ih we° k'ak-nyung.*
A teacher.	一位先生	*ih we° sien-sang.*
A doctor.	一位郎中	*ih we° laung-tsong.*
An unmarried woman.	一位小姐	*ih we° °siau-°tsia.*
A friend.	一位朋友	*ih we° bang-yeu.*

EIGHTEENTH CLASSIFIER, 張 (*tsang*), DENOTES SHEETS OF PAPER.

A sheet of paper.	一張紙	*ih tsang °tsz.*

A newspaper.	一張新聞紙	ih tsang sing-vung-°tsz.
A proclamation.	一張告示	ih tsang kau°-zz°.

NINETEENTH CLASSIFIER; 爿 (ban), DENOTES FIRMS, SHOPS, ETC.

A firm.	一爿行	ih ban ʻaung.
A foreign firm.	一爿洋行	ih ban yang ʻaung.
A shop.	一爿店	ih ban tien°.
A shop of foreign goods.	一爿洋貨店	ih ban yang hoo° tien°.
A pawn shop.	一爿典當	ih ban °tien-taung°.
A tea shop.	一爿茶館	ih ban dzo-kwen°.
A silk store.	一爿綢緞店	ih ban dzeu-doen° tien°.
A wine shop,	一爿酒店	ih ban °tsieu tien°.

TWENTIETH CLASSIFIER, 副 (foo°), DENOTES SETS OF THINGS.

A set of buttons.	一副鈕子	ih foo° °nyeu-°tsz.
A pair of bracelets.	一副鐲頭	ih foo° dzauh-deu.
A set of ear-rings.	一副圈	ih foo° choen.
A pair of spectacles.	一副眼鏡	ih foo° °ngan-kyung°.
A set of dominoes.	一副牌	ih foo° ba.
A set of dice.	一副骰子	ih foo° deu°-°tsz.
A set of chop-sticks.	一副筷	ih foo° kwʻan.
A set of tools or instruments.	一副傢生	ih foo° ka-sang.
A saddle and bridle.	一副馬鞍	ih foo° °mo-oen°.

TWENTY-FIRST CLASSIFIER, 雙 (*saung*), DENOTES PAIRS.

A pair of boots.	一雙靴	*ih saung hyoo.*
A pair of shoes.	一雙鞋子	*ih saung ʻa.°tsz.*
A pair of socks.	一雙襪	*ih saung mah.*
A pair of gloves.	一雙手套	*ih saung °seu-tʻau°.*

TWENTY-SECOND CLASSIFIER, 尊 (*tsung*), DENOTES IDOLS, AND A CANNON.

An idol (buddhist's).	一尊佛	*ih tsung veh.*
An idol.	一尊菩薩	*ih tsung boo-sah.*
An idol (tauist's).	一尊神道	*ih tsung zung-dau°.*
A cannon.	一尊砲	*ih tsung pʻau°.*

TWENTY-THIRD CLASSIFIER, 包 (*pau*), DENOTES BALES OF THINGS.

A bale of cotton.	一包花	*ih pau hwo.*
A bale of shirting.	一包洋布	*ih pau yang-poo°.*
A bundle of clothing.	一包衣裳	*ih pau i-zaung.*
A bale of medicines.	一包藥	*ih pau yak.*
A bale of tobacco.	一包烟	*ih pau ien.*
A bale of merchandise.	一包貨色	*ih pau hoo°-suh.*
A bale of silk.	一包絲	*ih pau ɛz.*
A bale of hemp.	一包麻絲	*ih pau mc-ɛz.*

FIRST LESSONS IN CHINESE.

Twenty-fourth Classifier, 棵 (k'oo), denotes trees, plants, etc.

A tree.	一棵樹	ih k'oo-zu°.
A flowering plant.	一棵花	ih k'oo hwo.
A plant of vegetables.	一棵菜	ih k'oo ts'e°.
A plant of wheat.	一棵麥	ih k'oo mak.
A plant of rice.	一棵稻	ih k'oo dau°.
A bunch of grass, etc.	一棵草	ih k'oo °ts'au.

Twenty-fifth Classifier, 面 (mien°), denotes flat objects.

A mirror.	一面鏡子	ih mien° kyung°-°tsz.
A flag.	一面旂	ih mien° ji.
A gong.	一面金鑼	ih mien° kyung-loo.
A drum.	一面鼓	ih mien° °koo.

Twenty-sixth Classifier, 堆 (te), denotes piles of things.

A pile of timber.	一堆木頭	ih te mok-deu.
A pile of fuel.	一堆柴	ih te za.
A pile of coal.	一堆煤	ih te me.
A pile of brick.	一堆碌磚	ih te lok-tsen.
A pile of stones.	一堆石頭	ih te zak-deu.
A pile of earth.	一堆泥	ih te nyi.
A pile of cloth.	一堆布	ih te poo°.
A pile of goods.	一堆貨色	ih te hoo°-suh.

TWENTY-SEVENTH CLASSIFIER, 綑 (°kw'ung), DENOTES BUNDLES OF THINGS.

A bundle of rattans.	一綑籐	ih °kw'ung dung.
A bundle of rice straw.	一綑稻柴	ih °kw'ung dau°-za.
A bundle of wood.	一綑柴	ih °kw'ung za.
One bundle.	一綑	ih °kw'ung.

TWENTY-EIGHTH CLASSIFIER, 管 (°kwen), DENOTES TUBULAR THINGS.

A flute.	一管笛	ih °kwen dih.
A flageolet.	一管簫	ih °kwen siau.
A gun.	一管鳥鎗	ih °kwen °'nyau-ts'iang.
A pistol.	一管手鎗	ih °kwen °seu-ts'iang.
A pen.	一管筆	ih °kwen pih.
A pencil.	一管鉛筆	ih °kwen k'an-pih.
A foot rule.	一管尺	ih °kwen ts'ak.
A steel yard.	一管秤	ih °kwen ts'ung°.

TWENTY-NINTH CLASSIFIER, 對 (te°), DENOTES A PAIR, A BRACE, ETC.

A pair of fowls.	一對雞	ih te° kyi.
A brace of ducks.	一對鴨	ih te° ah.
A brace of pheasants.	一對野雞	ih te° °ya-kyi.
A pair of pigeons.	一對鴿子	ih te° keh-°tsz.
A pair of candles.	一對蠟燭	ih te° lah-tsok.

A pair of candlesticks.	一對蠟檯	ih te° lah-de.
A husband and wife.	一對夫妻	ih te° foo-ts'i.

Thirtieth Classifier, 口 (°k'eu).

A book-case.	一口書廚	ih °k'eu su-dzu.
A ward-robe.	一口衣廚	ih °k'eu i-dzu.
A cup-board.	一口碗廚	ih °k'eu °'wen-dzu.
A coffin.	一口棺材	ih °k'eu kwen-ze.
A well.	一口井	ih °k'eu °tsing.

Thirty-first Classifier, 桶 (°dong), denotes casks, tubs, and buckets of things, etc.

A cask of wine.	一桶酒	ih °dong °tsieu.
A cask of ale.	一桶苦酒	ih °dong °k'oo-°tsieu.
A barrel of flour.	一桶乾麵	ih °dong koen-mien°.
A bucket of water.	一桶水	ih °dong °sz.
A keg of powder.	一桶火藥	ih °dong °hoo-yak.
A cask of butter.	一桶奶油	ih °dong °na-yeu.

Thirty-second Classifier, 瓶 (bing), denotes bottles, or vials of things.

A bottle of medicine.	一瓶藥	ih bing yak.
A bottle of wine.	一瓶酒	ih bing °tsieu.

A bottle of ale.	一瓶苦酒	ih bing °k'oo-°tsieu.
A bottle of vinegar.	一瓶醋	ih bing ts'oo°.
A bottle of oil, &c.	一瓶油	ih bing yeu.

THIRTY-THIRD CLASSIFIER, 箱 (*siang*), DENOTES BOXES OF THINGS.

A box of tea.	一箱茶葉	ih siang dzo-yih.
A box of sycee.	一箱元寶	ih siang nyoen-°pau.
A box of dollars.	一箱洋錢	ih siang yang-dien.
A box of materials.	一箱貨色	ih siang hou°-suh.
A box of toys.	一箱字相干	ih siang beh-siang° koen.

THIRTY-FOURTH CLASSIFIER, 封 (*fong*), DENOTES LETTERS, AND OTHER SEALED PARCELS, AS:

A letter.	一封信	ih fong-sing°.
An envelope.	一封信封	ih fong sing°-fong.
An official document.	一封文書	ih fong vung-su.

THIRTY-FIFTH CLASSIFIER, 幫 (*paung*), DENOTES A GUILD, A CLASS.

The literary class.	讀書幫	dok-su paung.
The mercantile class.	生意幫	sang-i° paung.
The Canton guild.	廣東幫	°Kwaung-tong paung.
The Ningpo guild.	甯波幫	Nyung-poo paung, or Nyung-pok paung.
The Nanking guild.	南京幫	Nen-kyung paung.
The entire guild or class.	一幫人	ih paung nyung.

THIRTY-SIXTH CLASSIFIER, 回 (*we*), DENOTES TIMES.

One time.	一回	*ih we.*
Two times.	兩回	°*liang we.*
Three times, etc.	三回	*san we.*

THIRTY-SEVENTH CLASSIFIER, 票 (*p'iau*°), DENOTES JOBS, ETC.

A job of work.	一票生活	*ih p'iau° sang-weh.*
A business transaction.	一票生意	*ih p'iau° sang-i°.*

THIRTY-EIGHTH CLASSIFIER, 樁 (*tsaung*), DENOTES AFFAIRS.

An affair.	一樁事體	*ih tsaung z°-°t'i.*
This affair.	第樁事體	°*di tsaung z°-°t'i.*
That affair.	伊樁事體	*i tsaung z°-°t'i.*
Two affairs.	兩樁事體	°*liang tsaung z°-°t'i.*

THIRTY-NINTH CLASSIFIER, 層 (*dzung*), DENOTES A STORY.

A three storied house.	三層樓	*san dzung leu.*
A seven storied pagoda.	七層塔	*ts'ih dzung t'ah.*

FORTIETH CLASSIFIER, 藏 (*dzaung°*), DENOTES THINGS PILED ONE ON TOP OF THE OTHER.

A pile of books.	一藏書	*ih dzaung° su.*
A pile of paper.	一藏紙頭	*ih dzaung° °tsz-deu.*
A pile of dollars.	一藏洋錢	*ih dzaung° yang-dien.*
A pile of clothes.	一藏衣裳	*ih dzaung° i-zaung.*
A pile of plates.	一藏盆子	*ih dzaung° bung-°tsz, etc.*

FORTY-FIRST CLASSIFIER, 股 (*°koo*), DENOTES SHARES IN BUSINESS.

One share.	一股	*ih °koo.*
A business of three partners.	一股分頭	*san °koo vung°-deu.*

FORTY-SECOND CLASSIFIER, 間 (*kan*), DENOTES ROOMS.

One room.	一間	*ih kan.*
A bed room.	房間　房頭	*vaung-kan, vaung-deu.*
A parlor.	客堂間	*k'ak-daung kan.*
An office.	寫字間	*°sia-z° kan.*
Shroff's room.	帳房間	*tsang°-vaung kan.*

FORTY-THIRD CLASSIFIER, 件 (°jien), DENOTES GARMENTS, PIECES OF BAGGAGE OR MERCHANDISE; ALSO AN AFFAIR; AS:

A garment.	一件衣裳	ih °jien i-zaung.
An affair.	一件事體	ih °jien z°-°t'i.
This affair.	第件事體	di °jien z°-°t'i.
That affair.	伊件事體	i °jien z°-°t'i.
Two packages.	兩件	°liang °jien.
Ten packages.	十件	zeh °jien.
Thirty pieces.	三十件	san-seh °jien.

FORTY-FOURTH CLASSIFIER, 埭 (da°), DENOTES ROWS OF THINGS.

A row of houses	一埭房子	ih da° vaung-°tsz.
A row.	一埭	ih da°.
A line of troops.	一埭兵	ih da° ping.
A row of trees.	一埭樹	ih da° zu°.
In a row, or line.	一埭生	ih da° sang.

Numerals with Classifiers.

In all the foregoing, the numeral *ih* has been used in the sense of the definite and indefinite articles, to denote singular objects. When it is desirable to speak of more than one object of either classifier, any other numeral may be substituted for *ih;* but the appropriate classifier must, in all cases, be introduced after the numeral; as:

Three men.	三个人	*san kuh nyung.*
Ten eggs.	十个蛋	*zeh kuh dan°.*
Four fowls.	四只鷄	*sz-tsak kyi.*
Twelve swords.	十二把刀	*zeh-nyi° °po tau.*
Nine knives.	九把刀	*°kyeu °po tau.*
Two roads.	兩條路	*°liang diau loo°.*
Six sticks of wood.	六根木頭	*lok kung mok-deu.*
Seven boards.	七塊板	*ts'ih kw'e° °pan.*
Three horses.	三匹馬	*san p'ih °mo.*
Eight books.	八本書	*pah °pung su.*
Seventeen doors.	十七扇門	*zeh-ts'ih sen° mung.*
Four letters.	四封信	*sz° fong sing°.*
Two hundred bales of silk.	二百包絲	*nyi° pak pau sz.*
Four hundred chests of tea.	四百箱茶葉	*sz° pak siang dzo-yih.*

Noun Omitted.

Thus the learner should apply any, or all of the numerals learned in the first part of this manual to any, or all of the classifiers, until he is perfectly familiar with their use.

If the object under consideration is present, or is perfectly well understood, omit the noun and simply use the numeral and classifier. Take the above examples.

Three.	三个	san kuh.
Ten.	十个	zeh kuh.
Four.	四只	sz° tsak.
Twelve.	十二把	zeh-nyi° °po.
Nine.	九把	°kyeu °po.
Six sticks.	六根	lok kung.
Two.	兩條	°liang diau.
Seven.	七塊	ts'ih k'we°.
Three.	三匹	san p'ih.
Eight.	八本	pah °pung.
Seventeen.	十七扇	zeh-ts'ih sen°.
Four.	四封	sz° fong.
Two hundred bales.	二百包	nyi° pak pau.
Four hundred chests.	四百箱	sz° pak siang.

PERSONAL PRONOUNS.

SINGULAR NUMBER.

NOMINATIVE CASE.	POSSESSIVE CASE.	OBJECTIVE CASE.
I. 我 °ngoo.	Mine. 我个 °ngoo-kuh.	Me. 我 °ngoo.
You. 儂 nong°.	Yours. 儂个 nong°-kuh.	You. 儂 nong°.
He, she, it. 伊 yi.	His, hers, its. 伊个 yi-kuh.	Him, her, it. 伊 yi.

PLURAL NUMBER.

NOMINATIVE CASE.	POSSESSIVE CASE.	OBJECTIVE CASE.
We. 伲 nyi°.	Ours. 伲个 nyi°-kuh.	Us. 伲 nyi°.
You. 倻 na°.	Yours. 倻个 na°-kuh.	You. 倻 na°.
They. 伊拉 yi-la.	Theirs. 伊拉个 yi-la-kuh.	Them. 伊拉 yi-la.

COMPOUND PERSONAL PRONOUNS, USED IN THE NOMINATIVE AND OBJECTIVE CASES.

SINGULAR NUMBER.

NOMINATIVE CASE.

I myself.	我自家	°ngoo z°-ka.
You yourself.	儂自家	nong° z°-ka.
He himself.	伊自家	yi z°-ka.
She herself.	伊自家	yi z°-ka.
Itself.	伊自家	yi z°-ka.

OBJECTIVE CASE.

Me myself.	我自家	°ngoo z°-ka.
You yourself.	儂自家	nong° z°-ka.
He himself.	伊自家	yi z°-ka.
She herself.	伊自家	yi z°-ka.
Itself.	伊自家	yi z°-ka.

PLURAL NUMBER.

NOMINATIVE CASE.

We ourselves.	伲自家	nyi° z°-ka.
You yourselves.	㑚自家	na° z°-ka.
They themselves.	伊拉自家	yi-la z°-ka.

OBJECTIVE CASE.

Ourselves.	伲自家	nyi° z°-ka.
You yourselves.	㑚自家	na° z°-ka.
They themselves.	伊拉自家	yi-la z°-ka.

EXERCISES IN THE PRONOUNS WITH A VERB AND A NEGATIVE.

It is mine.	是我个	°z¹ °ngoo kuh.
It is not mine.	勿是我个	'veh² °z °ngoo kuh.
My hat.	我个帽子	°ngoo kuh mau°-°tsz.
Your house.	儂个房子	nong° kuh vaung-°tsz.
It is yours.	是儂个	°z nong° kuh.
It is not yours.	勿是儂个	'veh °z-nong° kuh.

1. (*Z*°,) the verb to be. 2. ('*Veh*) not, no.

Is it, or is it not his?	是伊呢勿是伊个	°z yi nyi[3] 'veh °z yi kuh?
It is his (or hers).	是伊个	°z yi kuh.
It is not ours.	勿是伲个	'veh °z nyi° kuh.
We did not go.	伲勿去个	nyi° 'veh chi°[4] kuh.
Ours have not yet arrived.	伲个勿曾來	nyi° kuh 'veh-zung° le[6].
Where are yours?	哪个垃拉那里	na° kuh leh-la° °'a-°li?
Ours are on board ship.	伲个垃拉船上	nyi° kuh leh-la° zen laung°
They have not come.	伊拉勿來	yi-la 'veh le.
They have not yet come.	伊拉勿曾來	yi-la 'veh-zung le.
These are my own.	第个是我自家个	°di-kuh °z °ngoo °z-ka kuh.
It is not your own.	勿是儂自家个	'veh °z nong° z°-ka kuh.
It is his (or her) own.	是伊自家个	°z yi z°-ka kuh.
We went ourselves.	伲自家去个	nyi° z°-ka chi° kuh.
You yourself said so.	儂自家話个	nong° z°-ka wo°[7] kuh.
They came themselves.	伊拉自家來个	yi-la z°-ka le kuh.
You yourselves gave it me.	哪自家撥我个	na° z°-ka peh[8] °ngoo kuh.

The learner should not fail to run each of the above examples through all the persons of the pronoun, both singular and plural.

---

3. *Nyi*, or. 4. *Chi°*, to go. 5. *'Veh-zung*, not yet. 6. *Le*, to come. 7. *Wo°*, to speak. 8. *Peh*, to give.

INTERROGATIVE PRONOUNS.

Who? 啥 sa°?	Which? 那里 °'a °li?	What? 啥 sa°?

Sa° (啥), in the sense of *who*, is applied to persons, and only when we enquire after a person or persons wholly unknown; and is almost always joined to the noun.

Who? or Who is it?	啥人	sa° nyung?
Who said so?	啥人話个	sa° nyung wo° kuh?
Who did it?	啥人做个	sa°-nyung tsoo° kuh?[1]
Who took it?	啥人担个	sa°-nyung tan[2] kuh?
Who brought it?	啥人担來个	sa°-nyung tan le kuh?
Who has gone?	啥人去个	sa°-nyung chi° kuh?
Who wants it?	啥人要个	sa°-nyung iau°[3] kuh?
Who opened the door?	啥人開門	sa°-nyung k'e[4] mung?
Who shut the door?	啥人關門	sa°-nyung kwan[5] mung?
Who came?	啥人來个	sa°-nyung le kuh?
Who has been in?	啥人進來歇个	sa°-nyung tsing°[6] le hyih kuh?

Which, 那里 (°'a °li), is used to designate a certain number of persons or things, according to the numeral used before the classifier.

---

1. *Tsoo°*, to do. 2. *Tan*, to take. 3. *Iau°*, to want. 4. *K'e*, to open. 5. *Kwan*, to shut. 6. *Tsing°*, to enter.

Which one?	那里一个	°'a-°li ih kuh?
Which book?	那里一本書	°'a-°li ih °pung su?
Which road?	那里一條路	°'a-°li ih diau loo°?
Which shop?	那里一爿店	°'a-°li ih ban tien°?
Which two knives?	那里兩把刀	°'a-°li °liang °po tau?
Which three tables?	那里三只枱子	°'a-°li san tsak de-°tsz?
Which vessel?	那里一只船	°'a-°li ih tsak zen?
Which steamer?	那里一只火輪船	°'a-°li ih tsak °hoo-lung zen?
Which four doors.	那里四扇門	°'a-°li sz° sen° mung?

When the subject of conversation is present, or is well understood, the name or noun may be omitted, and simply the numeral and classifier may be used. Take the above examples.

Which one?	那里一个	°'a-°li ih kuh?
Which road?	那里一條	°'a-°li ih diau?
Which book?	那里一本	°'a-°li ih °pung?
Which shop?	那里一爿	°'a-°li ih ban?
Which two knives?	那里兩把	°'a-°li °liang °po?
Which three tables?	那里三只	°'a-°li san tsak?
Which vessel?	那里一只	°'a-°li ih tsak?
Which steamer?	那里一只	°'a-°li ih tsak?
Which four doors?	那里四扇	°'a-°li sz° sen°?

The learner should take many similar examples from the different classifiers, both with and without the noun, using different numerals.

Saᵒ (啥), in the sense of *what*, is used when the name, character, description and wants of persons or things, and the meaning and explanation of things, are enquired after: it usually follows a verb, and commences a sentence without a verb, as:

What name?	啥名頭	saᵒ ming-deu?
What is this called?	第个叫啥	ᵒdi-kuh kyauᵒ¹ saᵒ?
What occupation?	啥行業	saᵒ ʻaung-nyih?
What trade, or business?	啥生意	saᵒ sang-iᵒ?
What is the matter, or What business?	啥事體	saᵒ z̊-ᵒtʻi?
What business has he?	伊有啥事體	yi ᵒyeu² saᵒ z̊-ᵒtʻi?
What do you want?	儂要啥	nongᵒ iauᵒ saᵒ?
What does he want?	伊要啥	yi iauᵒ saᵒ?
What are you doing?	儂拉做啥	nongᵒ laᵒ tsooᵒ saᵒ?
What color?	啥个顏色 啥顏色	saᵒ kuh ngan-suh? saᵒ ngan-suh?
What kind or form?	啥个樣式	saᵒ kuh yangᵒ-suh?
What price?	啥價錢 啥行情	saᵒ kaᵒ-dien? saᵒ ʻaung-zing?
What o'clock?	幾點鐘	ᵒkyi ᵒtien-tsoong?
What news?	啥信息	saᵒ singᵒ-sik?
What weight?	啥分兩	saᵒ vungᵒ-ᵒliang?
What day?	啥日腳	saᵒ nyih-kyak?
What year?	啥年分	saᵒ nyien-vungᵒ?
What disease?	啥个病痛 啥病	saᵒ kuh bingᵒ? saᵒ bingᵒ-tʻongᵒ?

1. *Kyauᵒ*, to call. 2. *Yeu*, to have.

What did you say?	儂話个啥		nong wo° kuh sa° ?
What does he say?	伊話啥		yi wo° sa° ?
At what time?	啥辰光候	啥時	sa° zung-kwaung ? sa° z-'eu ?
What is your honorable name?	尊姓啥	尊姓	tsung sing° sa° ? tsung sing ?
What is the cause?	啥緣故		sa° yoen-koo° ?
What is the meaning?	啥解釋思	啥意	sa° °ka-seh ? sa° i°-sz ?
What is the use of it?	啥用頭		sa° yong°-deu ?
What place?	啥戶蕩化	啥場	sa° 'oo-daung? sa° dzang-hau° ?
What number?	啥數目		sa° soo°-mak?

Sa° (啥), with an interrogative, is also used in the sense of *any*, and, with a negative, of *no* or *none;* as:

Did you say any thing?	儂話啥否	nong° wo° sa° °va ?
I did not say any thing.	我勿話啥	°ngoo 'veh wo° sa°.
Does he wish to say any thing?	伊要話啥否	yi iau° wo° sa° °va ?
He does not wish to say any thing.	伊勿要話啥	yi 'veh iau° wo° sa°.
Have you any thing to say?	儂有啥話頭否	nong° °yeu sa° wo°-:leu °va ?
I have nothing to say.	我無啥話頭	°ngoo m-sa° wo°-deu.
Have you any prospect?	有啥望頭否	°yeu sa° maung°-deu °va ?
I have no prospect.	無啥望頭	m sa° maung°-:leu.
Have you any shirtings?	有啥洋布否	°yeu sa° yang-poo° va ?

I have.	有个	°yeu kuh.
I have none.	無沒	m-meh.
Have you any money?	儂有啥銀子否	nong° °yeu sa° nyung-°tsz °va?
Have you any employment?	儂有啥做否	nong° °yeu sa° tsoo° °va?
I have no business.	無啥做	m sa° tsoo°.
Has any one been here?	有啥人來否	°yeu sa° nyung le °va?
No.	無啥人	m sa° nyung.
Have you any plan?	有啥法則否	°yeu sa° fah-tsuh °va?
Is there any answer?	有啥回信否	°yeu sa° we sing° °va?
There is no answer.	無啥回信	m sa° we sing°.
Have you any other kind?	有啥別樣否	°yeu sa° bih yang° °va?
I have no other kind.	無啥別樣	m sa° bih yang°.
I have nothing more to say.	無啥別樣話頭	m sa° bih yang° wo°-deu.
Have you any thing to eat, (or drink)?	有啥吃否	°yeu sa° chuh °va?
I have nothing to eat.	無啥吃	m sa° chuh.

DEMONSTRATIVE PRONOUNS.

English	Chinese	Romanization
This, that.	第个　伊个	°di-kuh, i-kuh.
This man.	第个人	°di-kuh nyang.
That woman.	伊个女人	i-kuh °nyni-nyang.
This chair.	第把椅子	°di °po iui°-°tsz.
That table.	伊隻怡子	i tsak de-°tsz.
This road.	第條路	°di diau loo°.
That house.	伊座房子	i dzoo° caung-°tsz
This room.	第間	°di kan.
That door.	伊扇門	i sen° mung.
These two doors.	第个兩扇門	°di-kuh °liang sen° mung.
Those three windows.	伊个三扇窗	i-kuh san sen° ts'aung.
These four swords.	第个四把刀	°di-kuh sz° °po tau.
Those ten boxes.	伊个十隻箱子	i-kuh zeh tsak siang-°tsz.
Those ten boxes of tea.	伊个十箱茶葉	i-kuh zeh siang dzo-yih.

Apply the above, and similar examples, to all the classifiers, with different numerals: also the following examples, in which the noun may be omitted, as on page 26.

English	Chinese	Romanization
This one.	第个	°di-kuh.
These two.	第个兩隻	°di-kuh °liang tsak.
That one.	伊扇	i sen°.
Those three.	伊个三本	i-kuh san °pung.

These five.	第个五根	°di-kuh °ng kung.
Those ten.	伊个十把	i-kuh zeh °po.
These two pairs.	第个兩雙	°di-kuh °liang saung.
Those seven sets.	伊个七副	°i-kuh ts'ih foo°.
This boat, compared with that, is fast.	第隻船比之伊隻快	°di-tsak zen °pi-°tsz i-tsak kw'a°.

The study of the demonstrative pronouns, in connection with the different classifiers, with different numerals, will be a very profitable exercise.

INDEFINITE PRONOUNS.

All.	攏總	°long-°tsong
All, most (i e., men, or things, in general).	大概	da°-ke°.
Many, much.	多化	too-hau°.
Few.	少	°sau.
Each	每	°'me.
Each one, each man.	每人	°'me nyung.
Each kind.	每樣	°'me yang°.
Each (thing).	每件 每隻, etc.	°'me °jien, °'me tsak, etc.
Every.	各	kauh.
Every kind.	各樣	kauh yang°.
Every (thing).	各件 各隻, etc.	kauh °jien, kauh tsak, etc.
Whosoever, no matter who.	凡係人 勿論啥	van-i°, 'veh lung° sa° nyung.
Whatsoever, no matter what.	勿論啥 隨便啥 勿拘啥	'veh-lung° sa°, dzoe-bien° sa°, 'veh kyui sa°.
Whichever.	隨便	dzoe-bien°.
Others.	別个	bih-kuh.
Other men.	別人	bih nyung.
Other kind.	別樣	bih yang°.
Other forms, or styles.	別个樣式 別樣	bih-kuh yang°-suh, bih yang°.
Other places.	別處 別埸化	bih-ts'u°, bih dzang-hau°.

ADJECTIVES.

The adjective 好 (°*hau*) *good, well*, has a very wide application in Chinese. Indeed, every thing that is good, well, suitable, correct, charitable, palatable, ready, etc., and, in fact, every thing that suits the taste, or is agreeable to the mind, may be said to be 好 °*hau*.

The converse of nearly all the above may be expressed with equal latitude not by *bad*, but by *not good*, etc., 勿 好 '*veh* °*hau*.

Adjectives may be compared in Chinese.

The superlative may be expressed in different words; but this is regular; as:

Good.	好	°*hau*.
Better.	好點	°*hau tien*.
Best.	頂好	°*ting* °*hau*.
Bad.	邱	*cheu*.
Worse.	邱點	*cheu-tien*.
Worst.	頂邱	°*ting cheu*.
Cold.	冷	°*lang*.
Colder.	冷點	°*lang-tien*.
Coldest.	頂冷	°*ting* °*lang*.
In like manner compare		
Hot.	熱	*nyih*.
White.	白	*bak*.
Black.	黑	*huh*.
Green.	綠	*lok*.
Red.	紅	'*ong*.
Blue.	藍	*lan*.

English	Chinese	Romanization
Yellow.	黃	waung.
Short.	短	°toen.
Long.	長	dzang.
High.	高	kau.
Low.	低	ti.
Broad.	闊	kw'ch.
Narrow.	狹	ʻah.
Deep.	深	sung.
Shallow.	淺	°tsʻien.
Square.	方	faung.
Round.	圓	yoen.
Old.	老	°lau.
Young.	後生	°ʻeu-sang.
Fast.	快	kwʻaʻ.
Slow.	慢	manʻ.
Handsome.	趣	tsʻuiʻ.
Ugly.	怕	pʻoʻ.
Early.	早	°tsau.
Late.	晩	anʻ.
Heavy.	重	°dzong.
Light.	輕	chung.
Sharp.	快	kwʻaʻ.
Dull.	鈍	dungʻ.
Large.	大	dooʻ.
Small.	小	°siau.
Sweet.	甜	dien.
Bitter.	苦	°kʻoo.

Thick.	厚	°ṭcu.
Thin.	薄	bok.
Slippery.	滑	wah.
Hard.	硬	ngang°.
Soft.	軟	°nyoen.
Smooth.	光	kwaung.
Rough.	毛	mau.
Good, (moral).	善	°zen.
Wicked.	惡	auh.
Clear.	清	ts'ing.
Muddy.	渾	wung.
True.	眞	tsung.
False.	假	°ka.
Cheap.	强	jang.
Dear.	貴	kyui°.
Level.	平	bing.
Light.	亮	liang°.
Dark.	暗	en°.
Rich.	財主	dze-°tsu.
Poor.	窮	jong.
Wet.	濕	sak.
Dry.	乾	koen.

OF THE GENDER OF NOUNS.

I can trace but two genders in Chinese. When applied to mankind, the masculine is indicated by 男 *nen* and the feminine by 女 °*nyui;* as,

A man, a male.	男人	*nen-nyung.*
A woman.	女人	°*nyui-nyung.*
A male child.	男囝	*nen-noen.*
A female child.	女囝	°*nyui-noen.*
A male servant.	男相幫	*nen-siang-paung.*
A female servant.	女相幫	°*nyui-siang-paung.*

When applied to animals, the male is indicated by 雄 *yong* and the female by 雌 *ts'z;* as,

A horse.	雄馬	*yong* °*mo.*
A mare.	雌馬	*ts'z* °*mo.*
A male cow.	雄牛	*yong nyeu.*
A female cow.	雌牛	*ts'z nyeu.*
A cock.	雄雞	*yong kyi.*
A hen.	雌雞	*ts'z kyi.*
A male dog.	雄狗	*yong* °*keu.*
A female dog.	雌狗	*ts'z* °*keu.*
Male and female.	雌雄	*ts'z yong.*

OF THE PLURAL OF NOUNS.

The only way of forming the plural of nouns in Chinese, is either by prefixing a numeral indicating the number referred to, or by leaving off the numeral and classifier; in which latter case, the term is generic; as,

Men, mankind.	人	*nyung.*
Cows.	牛	*nyeu.*
Fowls.	鷄	*kyi.*
Forks.	叉	*ts'o.*
Books.	書	*su.*
Horses.	馬	°*mo.*

Or by prefixing a numeral; as,

Seven men.	七个人	*ts'ih kuh nyung.*
A hundred horses:	一百隻馬	*ih pak tsak* °*mo.*
About ten men.	十數个人	*zeh soo*° (or *su*°) *kuh nyung.*
Thirty or forty bales.	三四十包	*san sz seh pau.*
About a hundred.	百把	*pak po*°.
About a thousand.	千把	*ts'ien* °*po.*
About ten thousand.	萬把	*man*° °*po.*
A half dozen.	六个 六隻 六把	*lok kuh; lok tsak; lok* °*po*, etc.

A dozen.	十二个 十二隻 十二把	zeh-nyi° kuh; zeh-nyi° tsak; zeh nyi° °po, etc.
A dozen and a half.	十八个 十八隻	zeh-pah kuh; zeh-pah tsak, etc.
All men, or, men in general.	人人 大概人	nyung nyung; da°-ke° nyung.
Less than one hundred.	勿到一百 勿滿一百	'veh tau° ih pak; 'veh °men ih pak.
More than that.	勿罷	'veh °ba.

This term ('veh ba) is used in reply, where the person spoken to is conscious that the amount, or number given, or communicated by the person speaking, is short of what it ought to be; as,

More than a hundred men.	勿罷一百人	'veh °ba ih pak nyung.
There are more than fifty dollars.	勿罷五十洋錢	'veh °ba °ng-seh yang-dien.

The term 勿消 'veh siau may be taken as the reverse of 'veh ba, or the reverse of *more than necessary*, or *enough*; as,

Less than that.	勿消	'veh siau.
It is not necessary for so much as that.	勿消實蓋	'veh siau zeh-ke°.
Less than a hundred dollars.	勿消一百洋錢	'veh siau ih pak yang-dien.
Ten catties are more than are necessary.	勿消十觔	'veh siau zeh kyung, etc.

More than a hundred.	一百多	*ih pak too.*
More than a thousand soldiers.	一千多兵丁	*ih ts'ien too ping-ting.*
More than five hundred chests.	五百多箱	*°ng pak too siang.*
More than thirty rooms.	三十多間	*san-seh too kan.*
Near, (restricted to numbers).	毛	*mau.*
Near a hundred.	毛一百	*mau ih pak.*
Near fifty men.	毛五十人	*mau °ng-seh nyung.*
Near three *li*.	毛三里路	*mau san °li loo°, etc.*
One or more.	千把	*koen °po.*
A man or two.	千把人	*koen °po nyung.*
A dollar or two.	千把洋錢	*koen °po yang-dien.*

OF ADVERBS.

How?	那能　那亨能	°na-nung ? °na-hang°-nung ? as :
How do you know?	儂那能曉得	nong° °na-nung °hyau-tuh ?
How did you know?	儂那能曉得個	nong° na°-nung °hyau-tuh kuh ?
How did you do it?	那能做個	°na-nung tsoo°-kuh ?
How?	那能	°na-nung ?
How now?	現在那能	yien°-dze° °na-nung ?
How shall we manage it?	那能做頭	°na-nung tsoo°-deu ?
How can it be arranged?	那能做法	°na-nung tsoo°-fah ?
How did he manage to get in?	伊那亨能進來個	yi °na-hang°-nung tsing° le kuh ?
Why?	爲啥　爲啥咾	we°-sa° ? we° sa° lau ?
Why don't you (he or she) come?	爲啥勿來	we°-sa° 'veh le ?
Why did you (he or she) do it?	爲啥咾做個	we°-sa° lau tsoo° kuh ?
Why don't you (he or she) pay it?	爲啥勿付	we°-sa° 'veh foo° ?
Why do you (he or she) do so?	爲啥咾實蓋做	we°-sa° lau zeh-ke° tsoo° ?
Why is it?	爲啥咾	we°-sa° lau ?
When?	幾時	°kyi-z ?
When will you (he or she) come?	幾時來	°kyi-z le ?

When will you (he or she) do it?	幾時做	°kyi-z tsoo°?
When did you (he or she) go?	幾時去个	°kyi-z chi°-kuh?
When did you (he or she) do it?	幾時做个	°kyi-z tsoo° kuh?
How long since you (he or she) came?	來之幾時者	le tsz °kyi-z tse?
When is it due?	幾時期　幾時到期	°kyi-z ji? °kyi-z tau° ji?
Now.	現在	yien°-dze°.
I want it now.	現在要	yien°-dze° iau°.
I don't want it now.	現在勿要	yien°-dze° 'veh iau°.
Now it is too late.	現在來勿及	yien°-dze° le 'veh ji°.
Just now, a little while ago.	鉛鉛　勿多幾時	k'an-k'an (or k'ah-k'ah), 'veh too °kyi-z.
Quickly.	快快　快點　豪燥	kw'a°-kw'a°, kw'a°-tien, 'au-sau°.
Go quickly.	快點去	kw'a°-tien (or kw'a°-kw'a°) chi°.
Come quickly.	快點來	kw'a°-tien (or kw'a°-kw'a°) le.
Do it quickly.	快點做　做來快點	kw'a°-tien (or kw'a°-kw'a°) tsoo°; tsoo° le kw'a°-tien.
Be in a hurry.	豪燥　豪燥點　快點	'au-sau°, 'au-sau° tien, kw'a°-tien.
Only.	必過　只得	pih-koo; tsuh-tuh.
Only these two kinds.	只得第个兩樣	tsuh-tuh °di kuh °liang yang°.
Only small ones.	必過小个	pih-koo °siau kuh.

Thus, so, etc.	實蓋　實蓋能	zeh-ke°; zeh-ke°-nung.
Not so.	勿是實蓋能	'veh °z zeh-ke°-nung.
I want it so.	要實蓋個	iau° zeh-ke° kuh.
It is so.	是實蓋個	°z zeh-ke° kuh.
Very.	蠻	'man.
Very good.	蠻好	'man °hau.
Very fast.	蠻快	'man kw'a°.
Very high.	蠻高	'man kau.
Very large.	蠻大	'man doo°.
Very happy.	蠻快活	'man k'a°-weh.
Immediately.	就	zieu°.
Come immediately.	就來	zieu° le.
Do it immediately.	就做	zieu° tsoo°.
Return it immediately.	就還	zieu° wan.
Start immediately.	就動身	zieu° °dong-sung.
But.	但是　獨是　然而	dan°-°z, dok-°z, zen-r.
The man is honest, but he is good for nothing.	人是牢實但是無啥用頭	nyung z° lau-zeh, dan°-°z m-sa° yong°-deu.
But he cannot speak English.	但是伊勿會話大英話	dan°-°z yi 'veh we° wo° Da°-Iung wo°.
Verily, truly, indeed.	實在	zeh-dze°.
Moreover.	而且	r-°ts'ia or r-°ts'ien.
Not only.	勿但	'veh dan°.
He not only smokes opium, he moreover gambles.	伊勿但吃烟而且賭銅錢	yi 'veh dan chuh ien, r-ts'ia° °loo dong-dien.

Where?	那裏 啥戶蕩 那裏蕩 那 裏塊 啥所 那裏頭 啥 塲化	°'a-°li? sa° 'oo°-daung? °'a-°li daung? °'a-°li kw'e°? sa° °soo? °'a-°li deu? sa° dzang-hau°? etc.
Where are you going?	那裏去 到那 裏去	°'a-°li chi°? tau °'a-°li chi°?
Where did you find it?	啥戶蕩尋着个	sa° 'oo°-daung zing-dzak kuh?
Where is it to be bought?	那裏蕩有得買	°'a-°li daung° yeu tuh° ma?
Where are you?	儂拉那裏	nong° la °'a-°li?
Here.	此地 第塊	°ts'z-di°, °di-kw'e°, °di-deu.
I am here. It is here.	垃裏此地	leh-°li °ts'z-di°.
Men of this place.	此地人	°ts'z-di° nyung.
Bring it here.	担到此地來	tan tau° °ts'z-di° le.
It is not in use (current) here.*	此地勿行	°ts'z-di° 'veh 'ang.
There is a brisk trade here.	此地生意鬧猛	°ts'z-di° sang-i° nau° °mang.
We don't want it here.	此地勿要	°ts'z-di 'veh iau°.
There.	伊頭 伊塊	i-deu, i-kw'e°.
How is it there?	伊頭那能	i-deu °na-nung?
Is trade good there?	伊頭生意好否	i-deu sang-i° °hau va°?
Put it there.	放拉伊塊	faung° la° i-kw'e°.
Slowly.	慢慢點 慢慢 能	man° man° tien; man° man° nung.
Not so fast; go slowly.	慢點	man°-tien.
Walk slowly.	慢慢之走	man° man° tsz° °tseu.

* Literally, It is *no go* here.

Go up slowly.	慢慢能上去	man° man° nung °zaung chi°.
Distinctly.	清爽	ts'ing-°saung.
Speak more distinctly.	話來清爽點	wo° le ts'ing-°saung tien.
I do not see it distinctly.	我看來勿清爽	°ngoo k'oen° le 'veh ts'ing-°saung.
I do not hear it distinctly.	我聽來勿清爽	°ngoo t'ing le 'veh ts'ing-°saung.
Besides.	在外　另外	dze° nga° (we°); ling° nga° (we°).
Have you any besides these?	在外還有否	dze°-nga° (we°) wan °yeu va°?
There were five hundred soldiers, besides burden bearers.	有五百个兵在外還有挑點啥个	°yeu °ng pak kuh ping, dze°-we° wan° °yeu t'iau tien sa° kuh.
Inasmuch, seeing, still.	尚且	zang°-ts'ia, or zaung° ts'ia.
How much more?	何況	'oo-hwaung°.
If ye then, being evil, know how to give good gifts unto your children, how much more shall your Father which is in heaven give good things to them that ask him?	㑚有罪个人尚且曉得攏好物事拉儞个兒子何況㑚天爺倒勿肯攏好物事拉求伊个否	na° °yeu °dzoe-kuh nyung zang°-ts'ia hyau°-tuh peh °hau meh-z° la r-tsz, 'oo-hwaung° na° T'ien Ya tau 'veh °k'ung peh °hau meh-z° la° jeu yi kuh va°?
Still more.　Much more.	更加　越加	kung°-ka; yoeh-ka.
Much worse.	更加勿好	kung°-ka 'veh °hau.
Much longer.	更加長	kung°-ka dzang.
Still dearer.	更加貴	kung°-ka kyui°.
Still better.	更加好	kung°-ka °hau.

CONSECUTIVE CONJUNCTION.

Then, now.	難末	nan-meh.
Now it is well.	難末好哉	nan-meh °hau tse.
Finish this and then do something else.	做好之第个 難末做別个	tsoo° °hau-tsz °di-kuh, nan-meh tsoo° bih-kuh.
Now he is happy.	難末快活哉	nan-meh k'a°-weh tse.
Yesterday.	昨日　昨日之	zo (zau) nyih, or zo-nyih-tsz.
He went away yesterday.	伊昨日去个	yi zo-nyih chi° kuh.
He came to-day.	伊今朝來个	yi kyung-tsau le kuh.
The more you do, the more you will be able to do.	越是做越是會做	yoeh-°z tsoo°, yoeh-°z we° tsoo°.
For the time being.	且等	°ts'ia tung.

Too, OVER (denoting excess.) 忒 t'uh.

Too large.	忒大	t'uh doo°.
Too small.	忒小	t'uh °siau.
Too many.	忒多	t'uh too.
Too few.	忒少	t'uh °sau.
Too fierce.	忒兇	t'uh hyong.
Too stupid.	忒笨	t'uh bung°.
Too clever.	忒聰明	t'uh ts'ong-ming.
Too salt.	忒鹹　鹹	t'uh 'an.

Too young.	年紀忒輕	nyien° kyi t'uh chung.
Afterwards.	後首	°'eu-°seu.
Until.	直到	dzuh tau°.
Perhaps.	或者	'ok-°tse.
I fear.	恐怕	°k'ong-p'o°.
Daily.	日日　日多 日逐	nyih nyih, nyih-too, nyih dzok.
Openly, frankly, etc.	直落	dzuh-lauh.
Securely.	穩當	°'wung-taung°.
About.	約歸	iak-kwe.
About seventy bales.	約歸七十包	iak-kwe ts'ih-seh pau.
Secretly.	暗暗裡	en°-en°-°li.
Gently, with care.	輕輕能	ch'ung ch'ung nung.

OF PREPOSITIONS.

Above.	上頭	zaung°-deu.
Below.	下底　下底頭	°'au-°ti; °'au-°ti-deu.
Under, beneath.	底下	°ti-'au.
Inside.	裡向	°li-hyang.
Outside.	外頭	nga°-deu.
After.	後	°'eu.
Behind.	後底　後底頭　後頭	°'eu-°ti, °'eu-°ti-deu, °'eu-deu.
Before.	前　前頭	zien, zien-deu.
From.	打　打此地到伊頭	°tang; as, °tang °ts'z-di° tau° i-deu.
To (to arrive at).	到	tau°.
When did you arrive?	幾時到	°kyi-z tau°?
How many *li* from Shanghai to Peking?	打上海到北京幾里路	°tang Zaung°-°he tau° Pok-kyung, °kyi °li loo°?
On.	上	laung° (much used).
On the table.	枱子上	de-°tsz laung°.
On the chair.	椅子上	iui°-°tsz laung°.
On the floor.	地上　地欄上　地板上	di° laung°; di°-kauh laung°, di°-°pan laung°.
On the carpet.	地單上	di°-tan laung°.
On the ground.	地上	di°-laung°.
On the street.	街上	ka laung°.

On the way, or road.	路上	loo° laung°.
On the person.	身上	sung laung°.
On board ship.	船上	zen laung°.
On the foot, or leg.	脚上	kyak laung°.
On the hand.	手上	°seu laung°.
On the wall.	墙上	ziang laung°.
On the box or trunk.	箱子上	siang-°tsz laung°.
On the bed.	床上	zaung laung°.
On the window.	窗口上	ts'aung °k'eu laung°.
On the door.	門上	mung laung°.
On the head.	頭上	deu laung°.
On the roof.	屋上	ok laung°.
On a (the) plate.	盆子上	bung-°tsz laung°.
On shore.	岸上	ngoen° laung°.
On the water.	水上	°sz laung°.
In.	裡	°li (much used).
In Heaven.	天上	t'ien laung°.
In the box.	箱子裡	siang-°tsz °li.
In the drawer.	抽屜裡	ts'eu-t'i° °li.
In the house.	房子裡	vaung-°tsz °li.
In the parlor.	客會間裡 客堂間裡	k'ak-we° kan °li; k'ak daung kan °li.
In the dining room.	吃飯間裡 大茶間裡	chuh-van° kan °li; da°-ts'e° kan °li.
In the chamber.	房間裡 房頭裡 房裡	vaung kan °li; vaung-deu °li; vaung °li.
In the store room.	火食間裡	°hoo-zuh kan °li.

In the study.	書房間裡	su-vaung kan °li.
In the dressing room.	揩面間裡	k'a-mien° kan °li.
In the bath room.	淨浴間裡	zing°-yok kan °li.
In the office.	寫字間裡	°sia-z° kan °li.
In the compradore's room.	帳房裡	tsang°-vaung °li.
In the stable.	馬棚裡	°mo-bang °li.
In the field.	田裡	dien °li.
In the shop.	店裡	tien° °li.
In the hong.	行裡	ʻaung °li.
In the water.	水裡	°sz °li.
In the Winter.	冬裡	tong °li.
In the Summer.	夏裡	ʻau° °li.
In the Spring.	春裡 春上	ts'ung °li, ts'ung laung°.
In the Autumn.	秋裡	ts'ieu °li.
In the day.	日裡	nyih °li.
In the night.	夜裡	ya° °li.
In the church.	禮拜堂裡	°li-pa°-daung °li.
In the school room.	學堂裡	ʻauh-daung °li.
In the heart.	心裡	sing °li.
In the ground.	地皮裡	di°-bi °li.
In the grave.	坟山裡	vung-san °li.
In the well.	井裡	°tsing °li.
In hell.	地獄裡	di°-nyok °li.
In the go-down.	棧房裡	°dzan-vaung °li.
In the canal.	浜裡	pang °li.
In the river.	河裡	ʻoo °li.

In the city.	城裡	dzung °li.
In the temple.	廟裡	miau° °li.
In the ship's hold.	艙裡	tsaung °li.
In the eye.	眼睛裡	°ngan tsing °li.
In this month.	第个月裡	°di-kuh nyoeh °li.
In the ear.	耳朶裡	°nyi-°too °li.
In a (the) bottle.	瓶裡	bing °li.
In a (the) cask.	桶裡	°dong °li.
In the mouth.	嘴裡	°tsz °li.
In this.	第个裡	°di-kuh °li.
In that.	伊个裡	i-kuh °li.
In the wilderness.	荒野裡	hwaung-°ya °li.
In the light.	亮光裡　亮裡	liang°-kwaung °li; liang °li.
In the dark.	暗洞裡　暗裡	en° dong° °li; en° °li.
Within these two or three days.	第个兩三日裡	°di-kuh °liang san nyih °li.
In trouble.	苦惱裡　灾難裡	°k'oe-nau °li; tse-nan° °li.
In prosperity.	興發裡	hyung-fah °li.
In what?	啥裡	sa° °li?

CONJUNCTIONS.

English	Chinese	Romanization
Therefore.	所以　格咾	°soo-°i; keh-lau.
I had business, therefore did not come.	我有之事體所以勿來	°ngoo °yeu tsz z°-°t'i, °soo-°i 'veh le.
He is not honest, therefore I do not want him.	伊勿牢實　格咾我勿要	yi 'veh lau-zeh, keh-lau °ngoo 'veh iau°.
Also, still, yet.	也是　還	°'a °z, wan.
Also the same.	也是實蓋	°'a °z zeh-ke°.
Also a merchant.	也是生意人	°'a °z sang-i° nyung.
This also is a good one.	第个也是好个	°di-kuh °'a °z °hau kuh.
I also want to purchase.	我也要買	°ngoo °'a iau° °ma.
I also want to go.	我也要去	°ngoo °'a iau° chi°.
Do you still (or yet) want more?	還要否	wan iau° va°?
Though, although, notwithstanding.	雖是　雖然	soe-°z; soe-zen.
Although he is old, he is still able to work.	伊雖是老還做得動生活	yi soe-°z °lau, wan tsoo° tuh °dong sang-weh.
Because, for.	因爲　爲之	iung we°; we°-tsz.
Why did you run away?	爲啥咾逃走	we sa° lau dau °tseu?
Because I was afraid.	因爲我怕个	iung-we° °ngoo p'o°-kuh.
For this is the law and the prophets. (Matt. 7. 12.)	因爲律法咾先知是實蓋	iung-we° lih-fah lau sien-tsz °z zeh-ke°.
It is because matters are (were) thus, I do (did) not wish to have anything to do with it.	爲之實蓋我勿要搭講	we°-tsz zeh-ke° °ngoo 'veh iau° tah-kaung.

English	Chinese	Romanization
If.	若使　若然	zah-sz°; zah-zen.
That, so that.	等	°tung.
Then, well then.	難末　蓋末	nan-meh, keh-meh.
When you shall have finished this, then do that; or Finish this and then do that.	做好之第个難末做伊个	Tsoo° °hau tsz °di-kuh, nan-meh tsoo° i-kuh.
If he will not do as I propose, then what will he do?	若使伊勿肯照我蓋末伊肯做啥	zak-sz° yi 'veh °k'ung tsau° °ngoo, keh-meh yi °k'ung tsoo° sa°?
Lest.	省之	°sang-tsz.
Take an umbrella, lest you get wet.	担一頂傘省之淋濕	tan ih °ting san,° °sang-tsz° ling sak.
Neither, nor.	也勿	°'a 'veh.
Neither this nor that.	第个勿是伊个也勿是	°di-kuh 'veh °z, i-kuh °'a 'veh-°z.
In case, if, should.	倘使　倘然	t'aung° sz°, t'aung° zen.
Either, or.	或是	'ok-°z.
Either to-day or to-morrow.	或是今朝或是明朝	'ok-°z kyung-tsau, 'ok-°z ming-tsau.
And.	咾	lau.
The morning and evening.	早晨咾夜快	°tsau°-zung lau ya°-kw'a°.
Books, etc.	書咾啥	su lau sa°.

INTERROGATIVES.

? (general interrogative particle).	否	va°.
Have you found it?	尋着否	zing-dzak va°?

Meh 末—is used as an interrogative when you have reason to expect or hope for an affirmative answer; as,

Is breakfast ready?	飯好末	van° °hau meh?

Sa° 啥—as an interrogative, is sometimes found at the close, and sometimes at the commencement of a sentence; as,

What do you want?	儂要啥	nong° iau° sa°?
What price?	啥價錢	sa° ka°-dien?

°'*A-°li* 那裡—is also an interrogative.

Where are you going?	儂到那裡去 儂到那裡 那裡去	nong° tau° °'a-°li chi°? nong° tau° °'a-°li? °'a-°li chi°.

Nyi 呢—is also used as an interrogative.

Is it or is it not?	是呢勿是	°z nyi 'veh °z?
Is it good or not?	好呢勿好	°hau nyi 'veh-°hau?

WEIGHTS, ETC.

English	Chinese	Romanization
A picul.	一担　一百斤	ih tan°; ih pak kyung.
A catty.	一斤　十六兩	ih kyung; zeh-lok-°liang.
An ounce.	一兩	ih °liang
An ounce of silver.	一兩銀子	ih °liang nyung-°tsz.
1-10th of a *liang*.	一錢	ih zien.
1-10th of a *sien*.	一分	ih fung.
1-10th of a *fung*.	一厘	ih li.
1-10th of a *li*.	一毫	ih ʻau
Tls. 12.33.	十二兩三錢三分	zeh nyi' °liang san zien san fung.
Tls. 10.42.5.3.	十兩四錢二分五厘三毫	zeh °liang sz° zien nyi° fung °ng li san ʻau.
One dollar.	一元　一圓　一塊洋錢	ih nyoen, ih yoen, ih kʻwe° yang-dien.
A half dollar.	一个對開　半塊	ih kuh te° kʻe; pen° kʻwe°.
A quarter of a dollar.	一个四開	ih kuh sz° kʻe.
Ten cents.	一角	ih kauh.
One cent.	一分錢　一分洋	ih fung, ih fung yang-dien.
An inch.	一寸	ih tsʻung°.
1-tenth of an inch.	一分	ih fung.
A foot.	一尺	ih tsʻak.

Ten feet.	一丈	ih °dzang.
Ten feet square.	一方	ih faung.
A mow.	一畝	ih °m.
A foot square.	一尺見方	ih ts'ak kyien°-faung.

HOURS, DAYS OF THE WEEK, MONTH, YEAR, ETC.

An hour.	一點鐘	ih °tien-tsong.
Half an hour.	半點鐘	pen° °tien-tsong.
Quarter of an hour.	一刻	ih k'uh.
A minute.	一分	ih fung.
A day.	一日	ih nyih.
Sunday.	禮拜　禮拜日	°li-pa°, °li-pa°-nyih.
Monday.	禮拜一	°li-pa° ih.
Tuesday.	禮拜二	°li-pa° nyi°.
Wednesday.	禮拜三	°li-pa° san.
Thursday.	禮拜四	°li-pa° sz°.
Friday.	禮拜五	°li-pa° °ng.
Saturday.	禮拜六	°li-pa° lok.
A week.	一个禮拜　一禮拜	ih kuh °li-pa°, ih °li-pa°.
To-day.	今朝	kyung-tsau.
To-morrow.	明朝	ming-tsau.
Yesterday.	昨日	zau-nyih.

English	Chinese	Romanization
Day before yesterday.	過日子	koo°-nyih-°tsz.
Day after to-morrow.	後日	°'eu-nyih.
Two days.	兩日	°liang nyih.
Every day.	每日 日日 日多	'me nyih, nyih-nyih, nyih-too.
Day.	日	nyih.
Night.	夜	ya°.
In the day time.	日裡	nyih-°li.
In the night.	夜裡	ya°-°li.
In the morning.	早晨頭	°tsau-zung-deu.
In the evening (twilight).	夜快	ya° k'wa°.
In the evening (dusk).	黃昏動 黃昏頭	waung-hwung °dong; waung-hwung-deu.
In the forenoon.	上半日 上晝	°zaung-pen°-nyih; °zaung tseu°.
In the afternoon.	下晝 下半日 下晝動	°'au-tseu°; °'au-pen°-nyih; °'au-tseu°-°dong.
At noon.	日中 日頭直	nyih-tsong; nyih-deu-dzuh.
About midnight.	半夜把	pen° ya° °po.
First half of the night.	上半夜	°zaung-pen°-ya°.
The latter half of the night.	下半夜	°'au-pen°-ya°.
Just before daylight.	天亮快	t'ien-liang°-k'wa°.
Month, or moon.	月	nyoeh.
A month.	一个月	ih-kuh nyoeh.
A full month.	滿月	°men nyoeh.
This month.	第个月	°di-kuh nyoeh.
Last month.	前月	zien nyoeh.

Intercalary month.	閏月	nyung° nyoeh.
Next month.	下月	°'au nyoeh.
First of the month.	月頭　初頭	nyoeh-deu; ts°oo-deu.
On or about the first of the month.	月頭上	nyoeh-deu laung.
The end (or last) of the month.	月底	nyoeh °ti.
The middle of the month.	月半	nyoeh pen°.
Half a month.	半个月	pen°-kuh nyoeh.
Monthly, every month.	月月　月多　每月	nyoeh nyoeh; nyoeh-too, 'me nyoeh.
First day of the month.	初一	ts°oo ih.
Second day of the month.	初二	ts°oo nyi°.
Third day of the month.	初三	ts°oo san.
Fourth day of the month.	初四	ts°oo sz°.
Fifth day of the month.	初五	ts°oo °ng.
Sixth day of the month.	初六	ts°oo lok.
Seventh day of the month.	初七	ts°oo ts'ih.
Eighth day of the month.	初八	ts°oo pah.
Ninth day of the month.	初九	ts°oo °kyeu.
Tenth day of the month.	初十	ts°oo zeh.
Eleventh day of the month.	十一	zeh-ih.
The twentieth.	二十	nyi°-seh.
The twenty-first.	廿一	nyan°-ih.
Year.	年	nyien.
One year.	一年	ih-nyien.

Half a year.	半年	pen° nyien.
This year.	今年	kyung nyien.
Last year.	舊年	jeu° nyien.
Next year.	開年　來年	k'e nyien; le nyien.
The whole year.	一足年　足一年　滿一年	ih tsok nyien, tsok ih nyien, °men ih nyien.
Every year.	年常　每年　年多　年年	nyien dzang; 'me nyien, nyien too; nyien nyien.
First half of the year.	上半年	zaung° pen° nyien.
The last half of the year.	下半年	'au° pen° nyien.
The new year.	新年	sing nyien.
The close of the year.	年夜	nyien ya°.
The beginning of the year.	年頭上	nyien deu laung°.
From the beginning to the end of the year.	一年到頭	ih nyien tau° deu.
About a year.	年把	nyien °po.
After the new year.	過年	koo° nyien.

VERBS.

I am not aware that any attempt has ever been made to conjugate and inflect the verb in Chinese, through all its numbers, persons, moods and tenses, as it is done in English. As the attempt can not fail to be of great benefit to the student of the spoken language, I shall, at the risk of exciting a smile, try to throw some light upon this unexplored field.

Any one familiarly acquainted with any of the spoken dialects may, by close observation, detect in the Chinese stereotyped manner of conveying their ideas, certain forms of expression which change the sense of the verb with every variation of form, somewhat analagous to what we find in English, in the Indicative mood, Present, Imperfect, Perfect, Pluperfect, and Future tenses, also the Imperative mood and participle. The same forms may also be traced through all the tenses of the Subjunctive mood. Having tested this peculiarity in more than three hundred verbs, and finding that the moods and tenses are expressed in uniform manner, why may we not take this peculiarity of manner as a rule, inflect a verb through all its moods and tenses, and thus establish a rule for all other verbs that will be of infinite value to the student of the spoken language?

OBSERVATIONS ON THE MOODS.

The five moods, Indicative, Potential, Subjunctive, Imperative and Infinitive, may be distinctly traced in the Shanghai dialect. The Indicative mood, present tense, is only distinguished from the Imperative and Infinitive moods by the personal pronoun, expressed or understood.

The Potential mood prefixes to the verb such other auxiliary verbs as express possibility, liberty, power, will and obligation; as,

| You can go. | 儂可以去 | *Nong° °k'au-°i chi°.* |

They can come in.	伊拉可以進來	Yi-la °k'au-°i tsing° le.
He would not come.	伊勿肯來	Yi 'veh-°k'ung le.
He can (*has the physical power to*) do it.	伊能做	Yi nung tsoo°.
He can (*has the ability to*) do it.	伊會做	Yi 'we° tsoo°.
They ought to sell.	伊拉應該賣	Yi-la iung-ke ma°.
He must come.	伊總要來	Yi °tsoong iau° le.

The Subjunctive mood, which represents an action under a condition, supposition, etc., is preceded by a conjunction expressed or understood; or takes a suffix with the force of a conjunction; as,

If you do not assist, we cannot do it.	若使儂勿相幫伲勿能彀做	Zak-sz° nong° 'veh siang-paung, nyi° 'veh nung-keu° tsoo°.
If you do not find him, come back immediately.	若使儂尋伊勿着就轉來	Zak-sz° noong° zing yi 'veh dzak, zieu° °tsen le.
If it is finished, bring it.	若使好拉者擔來	Zak-sz° °hau la° tse, tan le.

OBSERVATIONS ON THE TENSES.

Five tenses may be traced in the Shanghai dialect: the Present, Imperfect, Perfect, and the Future.

The PRESENT TENSE has two distinct forms.

The simple; as, I eat.	我吃	°Ngoo chuh.
The progressive; as, I am eating.	我垃裏吃	°Ngoo leh-li° chuh.

The IMPERFECT TENSE has three distinct forms;
The simple; as,

I ate.	我吃个	°N*goo chuh kuh.*

The progressive form; as,

I was eating.	我垃拉吃	°N*goo leh-la*° *chuh.*

And the emphatic form; as,

I did eat.	我是吃个	°N*goo* °*z chuh kuh.*

The PERFECT TENSE; as,

I have eaten.	我吃者 我吃 拉者 我吃 過者	°N*goo chuh-tse,* or, °*ngoo chuh la*° *tse,* or, °*ngoo chuh koo*° *tse.*

The PLUPERFECT TENSE; as,

I had eaten.	我已經吃者 我已經吃拉 者 我已經 吃過者	°N*goo* °*i-kyung chuh tse,* or, °*ngoo i*°*-kyung chuh la*° *tse,* or, °*ngoo i-kiung chuh koo tse.*

The FUTURE TENSE; as,

| I will or shall eat. | 我要吃 | °Ngoo iau° chuh. |

THE IMPERATIVE MOOD.

| Eat. | 吃　吃上 | Chuh, chuh laung°. |

NUMBER AND PERSON.

Each tense of the verb has two numbers, the Singular and Plural, and each number has three persons, as in English; but the form of the verb of each person, both Singular and Plural, is the same; as,

SINGULAR.

1. I eat.	我吃	°Ngoo chuh.
2. You eat.	儂吃	Nong° chuh.
3. He, she or it, eats.	伊吃	Yi chuh.

PLURAL.

1. We eat.	伲吃	Nyi° chuh.
2. You eat.	㑚吃	Na° chuh.
3. They eat.	伊拉吃	Yi-la chuh.

CONJUGATION OF VERBS.

The verb may be conjugated in Chinese; as, present, *eat* 吃 chuh; imperfect, *ate* 吃个 chuh kuh; perfect participle, *having eaten* 吃子 chuh tsz°. It may be inflected as follows:—

INDICATIVE MOOD.

現時 PRESENT TENSE, SIMPLE FORM.

獨 SINGULAR.

1. I eat.	我吃	°Ngoo chuh.
2. You eat.	儂吃	Nong° chuh.
3. He, she *or* it, eats.	伊吃	Yi chuh.

衆 PLURAL.

1. We eat.	伲吃	Nyi° chuh.
2. You eat.	郍吃	Na° chuh.
3. They eat.	伊拉吃	Yi-la chuh.

現時行 PRESENT TENSE, PROGRESSIVE FORM.

獨 SINGULAR.

1. I am eating.	我垃裏吃	°Ngoo leh-li° chuh.
2. You are eating.	儂垃裏吃	Nong° leh-li° chuh.
3. He, she *or* it, is eating.	伊垃裏吃	Yi leh-li° chuh.

衆 Plural.

1. We are eating.	伲垃裏吃	Nyi° leh-li° chuh.
2. You are eating.	㑚垃裏吃	Na° leh-li° chuh.
3. They are eating.	伊拉垃裏吃	Yi-la leh-li° chuh.

不全 Imperfect Tense, Simple Form.
獨 Singular.

1. I ate.	我吃个	°Ngoo chuh kuh.
2. You ate.	儂吃个	Nong° chuh kuh.
3. He, *or* she, ate.	伊吃个	Yi chuh kuh.

衆 Plural.

1. We ate.	伲吃个	Nyi° chuh kuh.
2. You ate.	㑚吃个	Na° chuh kuh.
3. They ate.	伊拉吃个	Yi-la chuh kuh.

不全行 Imperfect Tense, Progressive Form.
獨 Singular.

1. I was eating.	我垃拉吃	°Ngoo leh-la° chuh.
2. You were eating.	儂垃拉吃	Nong° leh-la° chuh.
3. He, *or* she was eating.	伊垃拉吃	Yi leh-la° chuh.

衆 Plural.

1. We were eating.	伲垃拉吃	Nyi° leh-la° chuh.
2. You were eating.	倻垃拉吃	Na° leh-la° chuh.
3. They were eating.	伊拉垃拉吃	yi-la leh-la° chuh.

不全重 Imperfect Tense, Emphatic Form.

獨 Singular.

1. I did eat.	我是吃个	Ngoo° °z chuh kuh.
2. You did eat.	儂是吃个	Noong° °z chuh kuh.
3. He, *or* she, did eat.	伊是吃个	Yi °z chuh kuh.

衆 Plural.

1. We did eat.	伲是吃个	Nyi° °z chuh kuh.
2. You did eat.	倻是吃个	Na° °z chuh kuh.
3. They did eat.	伊拉是吃个	Yi-la °z chuh kuh.

全 Perfect Tense.

獨 Singular.

1. I have eaten.	我吃者	Ngoo° chuh tse.
2. You have eaten.	儂吃者	Nong° chuh tse.
3. He, *or* she, has eaten.	伊吃者	Yi chuh tse.

衆 PLURAL.

1. We have eaten.	伲吃者	Nyi° chuh tse.
2. You have eaten.	倻吃者	Na° chuh tse.
3. They have eaten.	伊拉吃者	Yi-la chuh tse.

La° tse and *koo°-tse* are frequently heard in the perfect tense; as, °*ngoo chuh la° tse*, or °*ngoo chuh koo°-tse:* the *la°* and *koo°* are not necessary to the sense.

加全 PLUPERFECT TENSE.

獨 SINGULAR.

1. I had eaten.	我已經吃者	°Ngoo °i-kyung chuh tse.
2. You had eaten.	儂已經吃者	Nong° °i-kyung chuh tse.
3. He, *or* she had eaten.	伊已經吃者	Yi °i-kyung chuh tse.

衆 PLURAL.

1. We had eaten.	伲已經吃者	Nyi° °i-kyung chuh tse.
2. You had eaten.	倻已經吃者	Na° °i-kyung chuh tse.
3. They had eaten.	伊拉已經吃者	Yi-la °i-kyung chuh tse.

La° tse and *koo° tse* are frequently found in the pluperfect; as,

°*Ngoo °i-kyung chuh la° tse*, or, *Ngoo °i-kyung chuh koo°-tse*.

我 已 經 吃 拉 者　　我 已 經 吃 過 者

未來 Future Tense.

獨 Singular.

1. I will or shall eat.	我要吃	°Ngoo iau° chuh.
2. You will or shall eat.	儂要吃	Nong° iau° chuh.
3. He will or shall eat.	伊要吃	Yi iau° chuh.

衆 Plural.

1. We will or shall eat.	伲要吃	Nyi° iau° chuh.
2. You will or shall eat.	哪要吃	Na° iau° chuh.
3. They will or shall eat.	伊拉要吃	Yi-la iau° chuh.

The learner should bear in mind that *iau°* has several meanings; as, *iau°*, to want; *iau°*, will or shall; *iau°*, must; and *iau°*, ought.

可 Potential Mood.

現時 Present Tense.

獨 Singular.

1. I may or can eat.	我可以吃	°Ngoo °k'au-°i chuh.
2. You may or can eat.	儂可以吃	Nong° °k'au-°i chuh.
3. He may or can eat.	伊可以吃	Yi °k'au-°i chuh.

眾 PLURAL.

1. We may or can eat.	伲可以吃	Nyi° °k'au-°i chuh.
2. You may or can eat.	哪可以吃	Na° °k'au-°i chuh.
3. They may or can eat.	伊拉可以吃	Yi-la °k'au-°i chuh.

SUBJUNCTIVE MOOD.

現時 PRESENT TENSE, SIMPLE FORM.

獨 SINGULAR.

1. If I eat.	若使我吃	Zak-sz° °ngoo chuh.
2. If you eat.	若使儂吃	Zak-sz° nong° chuh.
3. If he or she eat.	若使伊吃	Zak-sz° yi chuh.

眾 PLURAL.

1. If we eat.	若使伲吃	Zak-sz° nyi° chuh.
2. If you eat.	若使哪吃	Zak-sz° na° chuh.
3. If they eat.	若使伊拉吃	Zak-sz° yi-la chuh.

現時重 PRESENT TENSE, EMPHATIC FORM.

獨 SINGULAR.

1. If I do eat.	若使我是吃	Zak-sz° °ngoo °z chuh.
2. If you do eat.	若使儂是吃	Zak-sz° nong° °z chuh.
3. If he do eat.	若使伊是吃	Zak-sz° yi °z chuh.

衆 PLURAL.

1. If we do eat.	若使伲是吃	Zak-sz° nyi° °z chuh.
2. If you do eat.	若使哪是吃	Zak-sz° na° °z chuh.
3. If they do eat.	若使伊拉是吃	Zak-sz° yi-la °z chuh.

現時行 PRESENT TENSE, PROGRESSIVE FORM.

獨 SINGULAR.

1. If I am eating.	若使我垃裏吃	Zak-sz° °ngoo leh-li° chuh.
2. If you are eating.	若使儂垃裏吃	Zak-sz° nong° leh-li° chuh.
3. If he is eating.	若使伊垃裏吃	Zak-sz° yi leh-li° chuh.

衆 PLURAL.

1. If we are eating.	若使伲垃裏吃	Zak-sz° nyi° leh-li° chuh.
2. If you are eating.	若使哪垃裏吃	Zak-sz° na° leh-li° chuh.
3. If they are eating.	若使伊拉垃裏吃	Zak-sz° yi-la leh-li° chuh.

不全 IMPERFECT TENSE, SIMPLE FORM.

獨 SINGULAR.

1. If I ate.	若使我吃个	Zak-sz° °ngoo chuh kuh.
2. If you ate.	若使儂吃个	Zak-sz° nong° chuh kuh.
3. If he ate.	若使伊吃个	Zak-sz° yi chuh kuh.

眾 PLURAL.

1. If we ate.	若使伲吃个	Zak-sz° nyi° chuh k·h.
2. If you ate.	若使哪吃个	Zak sz° na° chuh k·h.
3. If they ate.	若使伊拉吃个	Zak-sz° yi-la chuh kuh.

不全重 IMPERFECT TENSE, EMPHATIC FORM.

獨 SINGULAR.

1. If I did eat.	若使我是吃个	Zak-sz° °ngoo °z chuh kuh.
2. If you did eat.	若使儂是吃个	Zak-sz° nong° °z chuh kuh.
3. If he did eat.	若使伊是吃个	Zak-sz° yi °z chuh kuh.

眾 PLURAL.

1. If we did eat.	若使伲是吃个	Zak-sz° nyi° °z chuh k·h.
2. If you did eat.	使使哪是吃个	Zak-sz° na° °z chuh k·h.
3. If they did eat.	若使伊拉是吃个	Zak-sz° yi-la °z chuh k·h.

不全行 IMPERFECT TENSE, PROGRESSIVE FORM.

獨 SINGULAR.

1. If I were eating.	若使我垃拉吃	Zak-sz° °ngoo leh-la° chuh.
2. If you were eating.	若使儂垃拉吃	Zak-sz° nong° leh-la° chuh.
3. If he were eating.	若使伊垃拉吃	Zak-sz° yi leh-la° chuh.

眾 PLURAL.

1. If we were eating.	若使伲垃拉吃	Zak-sz° nyi° leh-la° chuh.
2. If you were eating.	若使哪垃拉吃	Zak-sz° na° leh-la° chuh.
3. If they were eating.	若使伊拉垃拉吃	Zak-sz° yi-la leh-la° chuh.

全 PERFECT TENSE.

獨 SINGULAR.

1. If I have eaten.	若使我吃者	Zak-sz° °ngoo chuh tse.
2. If you have eaten.	若使儂吃者	Zak-sz° nong° chuh tse.
3. If he has eaten.	若使伊吃者	Zak-sz° yi chuh tse.

眾 PLURAL.

1. If we have eaten.	若使伲吃者	Zak-sz° nyi° chuh tse.
2. If you have eaten.	若使哪吃者	Zak-sz° na° chuh tse.
3. If they have eaten.	若使伊拉吃者	Zak-sz° yi-la chuh tse.

加全 PLUPERFECT TENSE.

獨 SINGULAR.

1. If I had eaten.	若使我已經吃者	Zak-sz° °ngoo °i-kyung chuh tse.
2. If you had eaten.	若使儂已經吃者	Zak-sz° nong° °i-kyung chuh tse.
3. If he had eaten.	若使伊已經吃者	Zak-sz° yi °i-kyung chuh tse.

眾 Plural.

1. If we had eaten.	若使伲已經吃者	Zak-sz° nyi° °i-kyung chuh tse.
2. If you had eaten.	若使哪已經吃者	Zak-sz° na° °i-kyung chuh tse.
3. If they had eaten.	若使伊拉已經吃者	Zak-sz° yi-la °i-kyung chuh tse.

The Verb TO BE.

This verb is irregular, and, in this dialect, restricted to *being in*, or *at* a place. 是 is generally considered to be the verb *to be*, but I can get nothing out of °z 是 but *yes*, or an affirmation. The idea of the verb *to be* is expressed, in this dialect, by 垃裏 *leh-li*°, if the person or thing is present; and by 垃拉 *leh-la*°, if it exists elsewhere, or if reference is had to something in the past.

Indicative Mood.

現時 Present Tense.

獨 Singular.

1. I am here.	我垃裏	°Ngoo leh-li°.
2. You are here.	儂垃裏	Nong° leh-li°.
3. He, she or it is here.	伊垃裏	Yi leh-li°.

眾 Plural.

1. We are here.	伲垃裏	*Nyi° leh-li°.*
2. You are here.	倻垃裏	*Na° leh-li°.*
3. They are here.	伊拉垃裏	*Yi-la leh-li°.*

不全 Imperfect Tense.

獨 Singular.

1. I was there.	我垃拉个	°*Ngoo leh-la° kuh.*
2. You were there.	儂垃拉个	*N'ong° leh-la° kuh.*
3. He, she or it was there.	伊垃拉个	*Yi leh-la° kuh.*

眾 Plural.

1. We were there.	伲垃拉个	*Nyi° leh-la° kuh.*
2. You were there.	倻垃拉个	*Na° leh-la° kuh.*
3. They were there.	伊拉垃拉个	*Yi-la leh-la° kuh.*

全 The Perfect Tense is not expressed by 垃拉 *leh-la°*, but by 到 *tau°*; as,

I have been here, or there.	我到歇者 我到過歇者	°*Ngoo tau° hyih tse,* or °*Ngoo tau° koo° hyih tse.*

獨 SINGULAR.

1. I have been here, or there.	我到過歇者	°Ngoo tau° koo° hyih tse.
2. You have been here, or there.	儂到過歇者	Nong° tau° koo° hyih tse.
3. He, or she has been here, or there.	伊到過歇者	Yi tau° koo° hyih tse.

眾 PLURAL.

1. We have been here, or there.	伲到過歇者	Nyi° tau° koo° hyih tse.
2. You have been here, or there.	㑚到過歇者	Na° tau° koo° hyih tse.
3. They have been here, or there.	伊拉到過歇者	Yi-la tau° koo° hyih tse.

不全 PLUPERFECT TENSE.

獨 SINGULAR.

1. I had been here, or there.	我已經到過歇者	°Ngoo °i-kyung tau° koo° hyih tse.
2. You had been here, or there.	儂已經到過歇者	Nong° °i-kyung tau° koo° hyih tse.
3. He, or she had been here, or there.	伊已經到過歇者	Yi °i-kyung tau° koo° hyih tse.

眾 PLURAL.

1. We had been here, or there.	伲已經到過歇者	Nyi° °i-kyung tau° koo° hyih tse.
2. You had been here, or there.	倻已經到過歇者	Na° °i-kyung tau° koo° hyih tse.
3. They had been here, or there.	伊拉已經到過歇者	Yi-la °i-kyung tau° koo° hyih tse.

倘 SUBJUNCTIVE MOOD.
現時 PRESENT TENSE.
獨 SINGULAR.

1. If I am here.	若使我垃裏	Zak-sz° °ngoo leh-li°.
2. If you are here.	若使儂垃裏	Zak-sz° nong° leh-li°.
3. If he or she is here.	若使伊垃裏	Zak-sz° yi leh-li°.

眾 PLURAL.

1. If we are here.	若使伲垃裏	Zak-sz° nyi° leh-li°.
2. If you are here.	若使倻垃裏	Zak-sz° na° leh-li°.
3. If they are here.	若使伊拉垃裏	Zak-sz° yi-la leh-li°.

不全 IMPERFECT TENSE.
獨 SINGULAR.

1. If I were there.	若使我垃拉	Zak-sz° °ngoo leh-la°.

2. If you were there.	若使儂垃拉	Zak-sz° nong° leh-la°.
3. If he, she, or it were there.	若使伊垃拉	Zak-sz° yi leh-la°.

眾 Plural.

1. If we were there.	若使伲垃拉	Zak-sz° nyi° leh-la°.
2. If you were there.	若使倻垃拉	Zak-sz° na° leh-la°.
3. If they were there.	若使伊拉垃拉	Zak-sz° yi-la leh-la°.

全 Perfect Tense.
獨 Singular.

1. If I have been here or there.	若使我到過歇者	Zak-sz° °ngoo tau° koo° hyih tse.
2. If you have been here or there.	若使儂到過歇者	Zak-sz° nong° tau° koo° hyih tse.
3. If he, she, or it has been here or there.	若使伊到過歇者	Zak-sz° yi tau° koo° hyih tse.

眾 Plural.

1. If we have been here or there.	若使伲到過歇者	Zak-sz° nyi° tau° koo° hyih tse.
2. If you have been here or there.	若使倻到過歇者	Zak-sz° na° tau° koo° hyih tse.
3. If they have been here or there.	若使伊拉到過歇者	Zak-sz° yi-la tau° koo° hyih tse.

全加 PLUPERFECT TENSE.

獨 SINGULAR.

1. If I had been here or there.	若使我已經到過歇者	Zak-sz° °ngoo °i-kyung tau° koo° hyih tse.
2. If you had been here or there.	若使儂已經到過歇者	Zak-sz° nong° °i-kyung tau° koo° hyih tse.
3. If he, she, or it had been here or there.	若使伊已經到過歇者	Zak-sz° yi °i-kyung tau° koo° hyih tse.

衆 PLURAL.

1. If we had been here or there.	若使伲已經到過歇者	Zak-sz° nyi° °i-kyung tau° koo° hyih tse.
2. If you had been here or there.	若使倻已經到過歇者	Zak-sz° na° °i-kyung tau° koo° hyih tse.
3. If they had been here or there.	若使伊拉已經到過歇者*	Zak-sz° yi-la °i-kyung tau° koo° hyih tse.

EXERCISES WITH VERBS, ETC.

Is he there?	垃拉否	Leh-la° va°?
He is there.	垃拉个　伊垃拉个	Leh-la° kuh; yi leh-la° kuh.
Where is he (or it)?	伊垃拉那裏　垃拉那里	Yi leh-la° °a li°? leh-la° °a li°?
He is in the office.	垃拉寫字間裡	Leh-la° °sia-z° kan °li.

* It would be better to use the character 哉 in place of 者 as used in conjugating the verb, retaining 者 for such expressions as 或者.—Ed.

If he is there, tell him to come here.	若使垃拉叫伊來	Zai-sz° leh-la°, kyau° (kau) yi le°.
To have.	有	°Yeu.
Have you it, or any?	儂有否	Nong° °yeu va°?
I have it.	我有哩　我有拉	°Ngoo °yeu li°; °ngoo °yeu la°.
I have some.	我有个	°Ngoo °yeu kuh.
I have it not.	我勿有	°Ngoo 'veh °yeu.
I have none.	我無沒	°Ngoo m-meh.
Have you any on board ship?	船上有否	Zen laung° °yeu va°?
No, none.	勿　無沒	'Veh; m-meh.
Have they any?	伊拉有否	Yi-la °yeu va°?
Neither have they any.	伊拉也無沒	Yi-la °'a m-meh.
Who has any?	啥人有个	Sa° nyung °yeu kuh?
No one has any.	禿勿有　無啥人有	T'ok 'veh °yeu; m sa° nyung °yeu.
How long have you had it?	儂有之幾時哉	Nong° °yeu-tsz °kyi-z tse?
I have had it over a year.	我有之一年多	°Ngoo °yeu-tsz ih nyien too.
To do.	做	Tsoo°.
To work.	做生活　做工夫	Tsoo° sang-weh; tsoo° kong-foo.
Can you do it?	儂會做否　做得來否	Nong° 'we° tsoo° va°? Tsoo° tuh-le va°?
I can do it.	我會做　我做得來个	°Ngoo 'we° tsoo°; °Ngoo tsoo° tuh-le kuh.
I can not do it.	我做勿來　我勿會做	°Ngoo tsoo° 'veh le; °Ngoo 'veh 'we° tsoo°.

Who can do it?	啥人會做	Sa° nyung we° tsoo°?
There is a Canton man who can do it.	有一个廣東人會做	°Yeu ih kuh °Kwaung-tong nyung 'we° tsoo°.
Call him to come and do it.	叫伊來做末哉	Kyau° (kau) yi le tsoo° meh tse.
Just now he is not able to work.	現在伊做勿動	Yien°-dze° yi tsoo° 'veh °dong.
Tell him to come and try it.	叫伊來做做看	Kyau° (kau) yi le° tsoo° tsoo° k'oen°.
Who did it?	啥人做个	Sa° nyung tsoo° kuh?
I did it.	我做个	°Ngoo tsoo° kuh.
He did it.	伊做个	Yi tsoo° kuh.
When can you do it?	幾時好做	°Kyi-z °hau tsoo°?
I can do it immediately.	就好做	Zieu° °hau tsoo°.
Wait a few days.	等兩日　隔兩日　歇兩日	°Tung° liang nyih; kak °liang nyih; hyih °liang nyih.
I cannot wait.	我等勿得	°Ngoo °tung 'veh tuh.
Are you at work on it?	垃拉做末	Leh-la° tsoo° meh?
When will you have it done?	幾時做好	°Kyi-z tsoo° °hau?
Within three days.	三日裡	San nyih °li.
Is it finished?	做好末　好末	Tsoo° °hau meh? °hau meh?
It is finished.	做好拉哉　好拉哉	Tsoo° °hau la° tse; °hau la° tse.
Not yet.	勿曾　勿曾哩	'Veh-zung; 'veh zung li°.
It will be done soon.	好快哉	°Hau kw'a° tse.
Not for some time yet.	未哩　未時　未拉哩	Mi° li°; mi° z; mi° la li°.

Do it quickly.	快點做	Kw'a°-tien tsoo°.
Will he do it?	肯做否	°K'ung tsoo°-va°?
He will not do it.	伊勿肯做	Yi 'veh °k'ung tsoo°.
Has he done it?	做末	Tsoo° meh?
He has done it.	做拉哉	Tsoo° la tse.
Why do you not do it?	為啥勿做	We°-sa° 'veh tsoo°?
Because it can not be done.	勿好做咾	'Veh °hau tsoo° lau.
It can be done.	好做个	°Hau tsoo° kuh.
I will try it.	我做起來看	°Ngoo tsoo° °chi le k'oen°.
If you do not do it well you will work for nothing.	做來勿好末白做个	Tsoo° le 'veh °hau meh, bak tsoo° kuh.
Of course.	自然	Z-°zen.
I will pay you when the work is finished.	生活做好之咾担銅錢	Sang-weh tsoo° °hau-tsz lau, tan dong-dien.
What can you do?	儂會做啥	Nong° 'we° tsoo° sa°?
I can do any thing.	樣色會做	Yang° suh 'we° tsoo°.
Have you ever done it before?	做過歇否	Tsoo° koo° hyih va°?
I have done it before.	我做過歇哉	°Ngoo tsoo° koo° hyih tse.
When will you begin?	幾時做起	°Kyi-z tsoo° °chi?
When did you begin?	儂幾時做起个	Nong° °kyi-z tsoo° °chi kuh?
How long since you commenced?	做之幾時哉	Tsoo°-tsz °kyi-z tse?
I have been at it a long time.	我做之多時哉	°Ngoo tsoo°-tsz ta-z tse.
When will you finish?	幾時做完畢	°Kyi-z tsoo° wen-pih?

I don't want to do it.	我勿要做	°Ngoo 'veh-iau° tsoo°.
You ought to do it.	儂應該做	Nong° iung-ke tsoo°.
You ought not to do it.	儂勿應該做	Nong° 'veh iung-ke tsoo°.
Don't do it.	勿要做	'Veh iau° tsoo°.
I am determined not to do it.	我定規勿做	°Ngoo ding°-kwe 'veh tsoo°.
Not allowable.	做勿得个	Tsoo° 'veh-tuh kuh.
It is allowable.	做得个	Tsoo° tuh kuh.
Not difficult to do; easy to be done.	好做　容易做	°Hau tsoo°; yong°-yi tsoo°.
Difficult to do.	難做个	Nan tsoo° kuh.
Spoiled (in making).	做壞哉	Tsoo° wa°-tse.
Do it well. It is well done.	做來好个	Tsoo° le °hau kuh.
It is badly done.	做來勿好	Tsoo° le 'veh-°hau.
To trade, or do business.	做生意	Tsoo° sang-i°.
A merchant.	做生意人　生意人	Tsoo° sang-i° nyung; Sang-i° nyung.
To write a composition.	做文章	Tsoo° vung-tsang.
To become a man.	做人	Tsoo° nyung.
To economize.	做人家	Tsoo° nyung-ka.
Can't afford to do it.	做勿起	Tsoo° 'veh-°chi.
He can afford it.	伊做得起个	Yi tsoo° tuh-°chi kuh.
To use violence.	蠻做　硬做	'Man tsoo°; ngang° tsoo°.
Don't be violent.	勿要蠻做	'Veh iau° 'man tsoo°.
The manner of doing (things).	做頭　做法	Tsoo°-dcu; tsoo°-fah.

How can, or shall it be done?	那能做頭	°Na-nung tsoo°-deu?
He has injured his own cause.	伊自家做自家	Yi z°-ka tsoo° z°-ka.
To defeat; to frustrate.	做脫	Tsoo° t'eh.
I could not accomplish it.	做勿成功	Tsoo° 'veh dzung-kong.
To act for another.	代做	De° tsoo°.
A substitute.	代做个	De° tsoo° kuh.
How much can you do in a day?	一日做得幾化	Ih nyih tsoo° tuh °kyi-hau°?
It can not be done in a day.	一日做勿及 一日做勿好	Ih nyih tsoo° 'veh-ji°; or Ih nyih tsoo° 'veh °hau.
He is not inclined to do it.	伊勿高興做	Yi 'veh kau-hyung° tsoo°.
To make clothes.	做衣裳	Tsoo° i-zaung.
A tailor.	做衣裳个 裁縫	Tsoo° i-zaung kuh; ze-vong.
To go.	去	Chi°.
I am going.	我去哉	°Ngoo chi° tse.
Has he gone?	去末	Chi° meh?
He has gone.	去哉	Chi° tse.
He has not yet gone.	伊勿曾去	Yi 'veh zung chi°.
Did he go?	去否	Chi° va°?
He went.	去个	Chi° kuh.
What has become of it (or him)?	那裡去哉	°A-li chi° tse?
Where has he gone?	到那裏去 那裏去哉	Tau° °a-li chi°? °a-li chi° tse?

Have you been?	去過末	Chi° koo-meh?
I have been.	去過哉	Chi° koo° tse.
Have you ever been?	去過歇末	Chi° koo°-hyih meh?
I have been once.	去過歇一回	Chi° koo°-hyih ih we.
How long have they been gone?	去之幾時哉	Chi° tsz °kyi-z tse.
They have been gone but a short time.	去得勿多歇 纔纔去	Chi° tuh 'veh too hyih; k'an k'an chi°.
They went long ago.	去之長遠哉	Chi° tsz dzang-°yoen tse.
You can go.	儂可以去 去末者	Nong° k'au-°i chi°; Chi° meh tse.
Go quickly.	快點去 要快點去	Kw'a°-tien chi°; iau° kw'a°-tien chi°.
Go together.	一淘去	Ih-dau chi°.
To go, or pass by; to pass over; to pass away.	過去	Koo° chi°.
Will you go? or are you going?	去否 去末	Chi° va°? chi°meh?
I will go; I am going.	去个	Chi° kuh.
What are you going for?	去做啥	Chi° tsoo° sa°?
Go and see.	去看	Chi° k'oen°.
I am going, or will go now.	現在就要去	Yien°-dze zieu° iau° chi°.
Depart; be off.	去罷	Chi° °ba.
Take it away.	拿去 担去	Nau chi°; tan chi°.
Take it with you.	帶去	Ta° chi°.
Is it safe or allowable to go?	好去否 去得否	°Hau chi° va°? chi°-tuh va°?

It is not safe or allowable to go.	勿好去　去勿得	'Veh-°hau chi°; chi° 'veh-tuh.
Not intimate; not on speaking terms.	勿來去	'Veh le chi°.
To eradicate.	去脫	Chi° t'eh.
I will not or do not go.	我勿去	°Ngoo 'veh chi°.
Go in.	進去	Tsing° chi°.
Not inclined to go.	勿高興去	'Veh kau-hyung° chi°.
O! go along.	去　去末哉	Chi°; chi° meh tse.
To come.	來	Le.
Come in.	進來	Tsing°-le.
He came in.	伊進來个	Ye tsing°-le kuh.
They have come in.	伊拉進來哉	Yi-la tsing°-le tse.
You had come in.	㑚已經進來哉	Na° °i-kyung tsing°-le tse.
Has he come?	來末	Le meh?
He has come.	來者	Le tse.
He has not come.	伊勿來	Yi 'veh le.
He has not yet come.	伊勿曾來	Yi 'veh zung le.
He will come.	來个　伊要來个	Le kuh; Yi iau° le kuh.
They will come in.	伊拉要進來个	Yi-la iau° tsing°-le kuh.
Let him, or them come in.	讓伊進來	Nyang° yi tsing°-le.
Tell him to come here.	叫伊來　喊伊來	Kyau° (kau) yi le°; han° yi le.
He will not come.	伊勿肯來	Yi 'veh-°k'ung le.
Come quickly.	快點來　就來	Kw'a°-tien le; zieu° le.

He will come soon.	來快哉　伊就來	Le kw'a° tse; Yi zieu° le.
I can not come.	我勿能彀來	°Ngoo 'veh nung-keu° le.
Come to-morrow.	明朝來	Ming-tsau le.
I have been here three times.	我來過歇三躺	°Ngoo le koo° hyih san t'aung°.
You can come; come ahead.	來末哉	Le meh tse.
To be on friendly terms; to correspond.	往來　來往　來去	°'Waung le; le °'waung; le chi°.
Hereafter.	將來	Tsiang le.
Originally, formerly.	本來　向來	°Pung-le; hyang°-le.
When will you come?	幾時來	°Kyi-z le?
When did you come?	幾時來个	°Kyi-z le kuh?
How long since you came?	來之幾時哉	Le-tsz °kyi-z tse.
Bring it here.	担來	Tan le.
Bring it with you.	帶來	Ta° le.
Come over.	過來	Koo° le.
Where is it from? Where are you from?	那裡來　啥所來	°'A-°li le? sa°-°soo le?
A new comer.	新來个	Sing le kuh.
Originally.	源來　本來	Nyoen-le; °pung-le.
Are they coming?	垃拉來否	Leh-la° le va°?
They are coming.	拉來哉	La° le tse.
Not time to accomplish an object within a given period.	來勿及	Le 'veh ji°.

Instigator.	來頭人	Le-deu nyung.
Whence does it emanate?	啥來聞 啥來頭	Sa° le-rung? sa° le-deu?
To eat; to drink; to smoke; to take medicine.	吃	Chuh.
To eat a meal.	吃飯	Chuh van°.
To drink tea.	吃茶	Chuh dzo.
To drink wine.	吃酒	Chuh °tsieu.
To smoke.	吃烟	Chuh ien.
To take medicine.	吃藥	Chuh yak.
Have you dined?	飯吃末	Van° chuh meh?
Not yet (eaten).	勿曾 勿曾哩 勿曾吃哩	'Veh zung; 'veh zung li°; 'veh zung chuh li°.
I am eating.	我垃裏吃	°Ngoo leh-li° chuh.
I was dining.	我垃垃吃飯	°Ngoo leh-la° chuh van°.
I have dined.	我吃哉	°Ngoo chuh tse.
I had dined.	我已經吃哉	°Ngoo °i-kyung chuh tse.
I don't want to eat.	我勿要吃	°Ngoo 'veh iau° chuh.
I am not able to eat; have no appetite.	吃勿落	Chuh 'veh lauh.
I can eat.	我吃得落	°Ngoo chuh tuh lauh.
I can not afford to eat it.	我吃勿起	°Ngoo chuh 'veh °chi.
He can afford to eat it.	伊吃得起	Yi chuh tuh °chi.
I can not eat it; do not fancy it; do not know how to go about eating it.	吃勿來	Chuh 'veh-le.
Dinner time.	吃飯勭	Chuh van°-dong.

Before dinner.	飯前	Van° zien.
After dinner.	飯後	Van° °·eu.
Food.	吃局　吃頭	Chuh jok; chuh deu.
To finish eating.	吃停　吃好	Chuh ding; chuh °hau.
Have you finished eating?	吃好末	Chuh °hau meh?
He has eaten it up.	吃脫哉	Chuh t'eh tse.
To get the worst of a bargain; to be cheated.	吃虧	Chuh chui.
To retain unlawfully; to appropriate to one's own use that which belongs to another.	吃過	Chuh koo°.
To suffer punishment; to get the worst of an affair.	吃苦	Chuh °k'oo.
If we make a living by serving another, we should obey his orders.	吃別人碗半由別人使喚	Chuh bih-nyung °'wen pen° yeu bih-nyung sz°-hwen°.
If the rations are not equal, the operatives will not put forth equal effort.	吃食勿幸勻相打勿齊心	Chuh zuh 'veh chien-yuin siang-°tang 'veh zi-sing.
To get drunk.	吃醉	Chuh tsoe°.
To eat enough; to eat to fullness.	吃飽	Chuh °pau.
Not enough to satisfy appetite.	吃勿飽	Chuh 'veh-°pau.
To be injured by eating.	吃傷　吃壞	Chuh saung; chuh wa°.
To be imprisoned.	吃官司	Chuh kwen-sz.
To ask; to inquire; to investigate.	問	Mung°.

English	Chinese	Romanization
I asked.	我問个	°Ngoo mung° kuh.
I have asked.	我問拉哉	°Ngoo mung° la° tse.
I had asked.	我已經問過哉	°Ngoo °i-kyung mung° koo° tse.
I will ask.	我要問	°Ngoo iau° mung°.
Ask him.	問伊	Mung° yi.
Inquire the way.	問路	Mung° loo°.
I beg to ask, or inquire.	請問	°Ts'ing mung°.
Inquire of others.	問別人	Mung° bih-nyung°.
Did you ask?	問否	Mung° va°?
I did not ask.	我勿問	°Ngoo 'veh mung°.
Why did you not inquire?	爲啥勿問	We°-sa° 'veh mung°?
Go and inquire, or ask.	去問	Chi° mung°.
Make definite inquiries.	問清爽	Mung° ts'ing-°saung.
Unable to get information by inquiries.	問勿出	Mung° 'veh ts'eh.
To judge, to try a person, or case.	審問	°Sung-mung°.
Have you ever inquired?	問歇否	Mung° hyih va°?
I have inquired.	我問過歇哉	°Ngoo mung° koo° kyih tse.
I will make inquiries about it.	我要問問看	°Ngoo iau° mung° mung° k'oen°.
I have inquired everywhere.	各處問到家哉	Kauh-ts'u° mung° tau° ka tse.
It is not necessary to inquire.	勿要問得勿必問得	'Veh iau° mung° tuh; 'veh pih mung° tuh.
To speak; to say.	話	Wo°.
I said so.	我話个	°Ngoo° wo° kuh.

I have spoken.	我話拉哉	°Ngoo wo° la° tse.
I had spoken.	我已經話拉哉	°Ngoo °i-kyung wo° la° tse.
I will or shall tell.	我要話个	°Ngoo iau° wo° kuh.
I did say so.	我是話个	°Ngoo °z wo° kuh.
I did not say so.	我是勿話个	°Ngoo °z 'veh wo° kuh.
Don't say anything about it.	勿要話開來	'Veh iau° wo° k'e le.
I will not speak of it.	我勿話	°Ngoo 'veh wo°.
Who said so?	啥人話个	Sa° nyung wo° kuh?
You said so.	儂話个	Nong° wo° kuh.
What did or do you say?	儂話啥	Nong° wo° sa°?
I did not say anything.	我勿話啥	°Ngoo 'veh wo° sa°.
You told me so.	儂對我話个	Nong° te° °ngoo wo° kuh.
When did I tell you?	我幾時對儂話	°Ngoo °kyi-z te° °nong wo°?
Able to speak (as a language).	會話　話得來	'We° wo°; wo° tuh le.
Unable to speak.	勿會話　話勿來	'Veh 'we° wo°; wo° 'veh le.
I can not speak Chinese.	中國話我話勿來	Tsong-kok wo°, °ngoo wo° 'veh le.
You can speak it.	儂話得來个	Nong° wo° tuh le kuh.
You must speak the truth.	要話牢實話話眞話	Iau° wo° lau-zeh wo°; wo° tsung wo°.
Don't use violent language.	勿要話蠻話	'Veh iau° wo°; 'man wo°.
Don't be so noisy.	勿要鬧來死	'Veh iau° nau° le° °si.
A sentence; a word.	一句說話	Ih kyui seh-wo°.

English	Chinese	Romanization
What are you talking about?	儂拉話啥	°Nong la wo° sa°?
To speak evil.	話邱話	Wo° cheu wo°.
Don't slander people.	勿要話瘵別人	'Veh iau° wo°-°liau bih nyung.
There was not time to speak.	來勿及話	Le 'veh ji° wo°.
Flattering words.	客話 客氣話頭	K'ak wo°; k'ak-chi° wo°-deu.
Words spoken in vain.	白話脫	Bak-wo° t'eh.
Laughable words; words to amuse children.	笑話	Siau° wo°.
Idle words.	閒話	°'An wo°.
Can not reconcile them.	話勿理	Wo° 'veh-°li.
It is not necessary to say anything.	勿要話得 勿必話得	'Veh iau° wo° tuh; 'veh pih wo° tuh.
Boastful words.	大話	Doo° wo°.
False or imaginary words.	妄話	Maung° wo°.
To buy.	買	°Ma.
I bought it.	我買个 我買拉个	°Ngoo °ma kuh; °ngoo °ma la° kuh.
I did buy it.	我是買个	°Ngoo °z °ma kuh.
I am buying now.	我現在垃裏買	°Ngoo yien°-dze° leh-li °ma.
I was buying.	我垃拉買	°Ngoo leh-la° °ma.
I have bought.	我買拉哉	°Ngoo °ma la° tse.
I had bought.	我已經買拉哉	°Ngoo °i-kyung °ma la° tse.
I want to purchase.	我要買	°Ngoo iau° °ma.

How much do you want?	儂要買幾化	Nong° iau° °ma °kyi-hau°?
I do not wish to purchase.	我勿要買	°Ngoo 'veh-iau° °ma.
Do you wish to purchase?	儂要買否　要買否	Nong° iau° °ma va°? Iau° °ma va°?
Buy it.	買末哉	°Ma meh-tse.
It can be bought.	好買个	°Hau °ma kuh.
No where to be had.	無買處　買勿着	M °ma t'su°; °ma 'veh dzak.
It is to be had.	有買處	Yeu° °ma t'su°.
It can not be bought at that price.	買勿動	°Ma 'veh °dong.
It can be bought at that price.	買得動	°Ma tuh-°dong.
Go and buy.	去買	Chi° °ma.
To make a few purchases.	買點啥　買物事	°Ma tien sa°; °ma meh-z.
Where did you buy it?	那裏頭買着个	°'A-li°-deu °ma-dzak kuh?
Have you bought?	買拉末	°Ma la° meh?
I have bought.	買拉哉	°Ma la° tse.
I have not yet bought.	我勿曾買	°Ngoo 'veh-zung °ma.
At what price did you buy?	儂買來啥價錢　幾錢買个	Nong° °ma le sa° ka°-dien? °Kyi dien °ma kuh?
Bought at a moderate price.	買來强	°Ma le jang.
Paid a high price.	買來貴	°Ma le kyui°.
Can not afford to buy.	買勿起	°Ma 'veh °chi.

English	Chinese	Romanization
Can afford it.	買得起	°Ma tuh °chi.
Did not succeed in buying.	買勿成功	°Ma 'veh dzung-kong.
I want to buy more.	我還要買	°Ngoo wan iau° °ma.
Is it to be had?	有得買否	°Yeu tuh °ma va°?
It is to be had.	有得買个 有个	°Yeu tuh °ma kuh; °yeu kuh.
Why don't you purchase?	爲啥勿買	We sa° 'veh °ma?
He don't know how to buy.	伊買勿來	Yi °ma 'veh lc.
Not necessary to buy.	勿必買	'Veh pih °ma.
Invoice price.	買價	°Ma kz°.
How much have you bought?	買之幾好	°Ma tsz °kyi-°hau?
I have not bought much.	買得勿多	°Ma tuh 'veh too.
Try to purchase.	買買看	°Ma °ma k'oen°.
To sell.	賣 賣脫	Ma°; ma°-t'eh.
I sold it.	我賣脫个	°Ngoo ma°-t'eh kuh.
I have sold it.	我賣脫哉	°Ngoo ma°-t'eh tse.
I had sold it.	我已經賣脫哉	°Ngoo °i-kyung ma°-t'eh tse.
Will you sell it?	賣否 要賣否	Ma° va°? iau° ma° va°?
Is it for sale? I will sell it. It is for sale.	賣个	Ma° kuh.
I will dispose of it.	我要賣脫伊	°Ngoo iau° ma°-t'eh yi.
I can not sell it.	我賣勿脫	°Ngoo ma° 'veh t'eh.
Have you sold it?	賣脫末	Ma° t'eh meh?

English	Chinese	Romanization
To whom did you sell?	賣拉啥人	°Ma la° sa° nyung?
I have sold all.	賣完哉	Ma° wen tse.
To sell at auction.	拍賣	P'ak ma°.
It was sold at auction.	拍賣脫	P'ak ma°-t'eh.
I can not sell at that price.	賣勿動	Ma° 'veh °dong.
I will not sell (at that price).	勿賣	'Veh ma°.
Selling price.	賣價	Ma° ka°.
To give; to transmit by hand; to yield to the power of; to give in marriage.	撥	Peh.
Give, or hand it to me.	撥我　撥拉我	Peh °ngoo; peh la° °ngoo.
I shall not give, or hand it.	我勿撥	°Ngoo 'veh peh.
He is not willing to give.	伊勿肯撥	Yi 'veh °k'ung peh.
I gave, or handed it to him.	我撥伊个　我撥拉伊	°Ngoo peh yi kuh; °ngoo peh la° yi.
Who gave it to you?	啥人撥儂	Sa° nyung peh nong°?
I have given it.	我撥拉哉	°Ngoo peh la° tse.
I have given it away.	我撥脫哉	°Ngoo peh t'eh tse.
Give me notice, or warning.	撥信我	Peh sing° °ngoo.
I endured a beating from him.	我撥伊打	°Ngoo peh yi °tang.
Don't allow him to have it. Don't give it to him.	勿要撥伊	'Veh iau° peh yi.
I have already given it to him; I had given it to him.	我已經撥拉哉	°Ngoo °i-kyung peh la° tse.

Give him something to eat.	撥點啥拉伊吃	*Peh tien sa° la° yi chuh.*
When will you give it to me?	儂幾時撥我	*Nong° °kyi-z peh °ngoo?*
I will hand it to you to-morrow.	明朝撥儂	*Ming-tsau peh nong°.*
To pay money.	付	*Foo°.*
I paid it.	我付个	*°Ngoo foo° kuh.*
I have paid it.	我付拉哉	*°Ngoo foo° la° tse.*
I have already paid it; I had paid it.	我已經付拉哉	*°Ngoo °i-kyung foo° la° tse.*
Pay it.	付末哉	*Foo° meh tse.*
To pay out.	付出　付出去	*Foo°-ts'eh; foo°-ts'eh chi°.*
To pay in.	付進來　付下來	*Foo° tsing° le; foo° °'au le.*
Not able to pay.	付勿出	*Foo° 'veh ts'eh.*
Able to pay.	付得出	*Foo° tuh ts'eh.*
Has he paid it?	付拉末	*Foo° la° meh?*
He has not yet paid?	伊勿曾付	*Yi 'veh-zung foo°.*
When will you pay me?	幾時付拉我	*°Kyi-z foo° la °ngoo?*
When did you pay?	幾時付个	*°Kyi-z foo° kuh?*
Tell him to pay.	叫伊付下去	*Kau yi foo° °'au chi°.*
Ask him to pay.	叫伊付下來	*Kau yi foo° °'au le.*
How much money is to be paid out to-day?	今朝要付出去幾化銀子	*Kyung-tsau iau° foo° ts'eh chi° °kyi-hau nyung°-tsz?*
To whom did you pay it?	儂付拉啥人	*Nong° foo° lu° sa° nyung?*
I have paid it out.	我付脫哉	*°Ngoo foo° t'eh tse.*

Unable to pay now.	現在付勿出	Yien°-dze° foo° 'veh ts'eh.
To pay in full.	付清	Foo° ts'ing.
To receive; to collect.	收	Seu.
To collect accounts.	收賬	Seu tsang°.
To receive payment for a lease.	收租	Seu tsoo.
To receive house rent.	收房租　收房錢	Seu vaung-tsoo; seu vaung-dien.
To receive payment in kind.	收租米	Seu tsoo °mi.
I have received payment in full.	收清拉哉	Seu ts'ing la° tse.
Did you receive it?	收着否	Seu dzak va°?
I did not receive it.	我收勿着	°Ngoo seu 'veh dzak.
I did receive it.	我收着个	°Ngoo seu dzak kuh.
I did not receive anything.	我收勿着啥	°Ngoo seu 'veh dzak sa°.
A receipt.	收票	Seu p'iau°.
To finish or complete a work.	收場	Seu dzang.
A receipt in full.	收清票	Seu ts'ing p'iau°.
To suffer imprisonment.	收監	Seu kan.
To entertain one in distress.	收留	Seu lieu.
To clean up, to arrange things.	收拾好	Seu zeh °hau.
To make a clean sweep of things.	收括	Seu kwah.
To draw tight (as a cord).	收緊	Seu °kyung.
Draw it tight.	收來緊	Seu le °kyung.

To build.	造	°Zau.
To build a house.	造房子	°Zau vaung-°tsz.
To build a bridge.	造一條橋	°Zau ih-diau jau.
To build a boat, or vessel.	造船	°Zau zen.
To cast a gun.	造砲　鑄砲	°Zau p'au°; tsu° p'au°.
To erect a battery.	造砲臺	°Zau p'au°-de.
To take census.	造册子	°Zau ts'ak-°tsz.
To start a rumor.	造謠言	°Zau yau-yien.
Have you completed your house?	房子造好末	Vaung°-tsz °zau °hau meh?
It is finished.	造好哉	°Zau °hau tse.
To build a city wall.	造城頭	°Zau dzung-deu.
To build a wall.	砌墻	Ts'i° ziang.
To build a single brick partition.	砌壁	T'si° pih.
To pave a road.	砌街	T'si° ka.
To sit.	坐	°Zoo.
Please be seated.	請坐	°Ts'ing °zoo.
Sit down; be seated.	坐坐	°Zoo °zoo.
Sit a while.	坐一歇	°Zoo ih hyih.
I don't wish to sit.	勿要坐	'Veh iau° °zoo.
I have no time to sit.	我無功夫坐	°Ngoo m kong-foo °zoo.
Not room to sit, or be seated.	坐勿落	°Zoo 'veh lauh.
Sit still.	坐拉	°Zoo la°.
Sit on it.	坐拉上	°Zoo la° laung°.
Room to sit, or be seated.	坐得落	°Zoo tuh lauh.

Cushion for a seat.	坐褥	°Zoo-nyok.
To sit on a seat of judgment.	坐堂	°Zoo daung.
A throne.	坐位	°Zoo-we°.
To stand.	立	Lih.
Stand; stand still; is, or was standing.	立拉	Lih la°.
Stand up; stand it on end.	立起來	Lih °chi le.
Can not stand; unable to stand.	立勿動	Lih 'veh °dong.
Can not stand against such odds; can not bear such losses.	立勿住	Lih 'veh dzu°.
Can stand, etc.	立得住	Lih tuh dzu°.
Stand to one side.	立拉邊頭	Lih la° pien-deu.
To know.	曉得	°Hyau-tuh.
Do you know.	曉得否　曉得勿曉得	°Hyau-tuh va°? °Hyau-tuh 'veh °hyau-tuh?
Do not know.	勿曉得	'Veh °hyau-tuh.
I know.	我曉得	°Ngoo °hyau-tuh.
I knew it.	我曉得个	°Ngoo °hyau-tuh kuh.
I have known it.	我曉得拉哉	°Ngoo °hyau-tuh la° tse.
I had known it.	我已經曉得拉哉	°Ngoo °i-kyung °hyau-tuh la° tse.
How long have you known it?	儂曉得之幾時哉	Nong° °hyau-tuh-tsz °kyi-z tse?
I have known it a long time.	我曉得之長遠哉	°Ngoo °hyau-tuh-tsz dzang °yoen tse.

I have known it but a short time.	我曉得勿多幾時 鉛曉得	°Ngoo °hyau-tuh 'veh too °kyi-z, k'an °hyau-tuh.
I have always known it.	我一向曉得个	°Ngoo ih-hyang° °hyau-tuh kuh.
I know a little about it.	曉得點 有點曉得	°Hyau-tuh tien; °yeu tien °hyau-tuh.
I know all about it.	我禿曉得	°Ngoo t'ok °hyau tuh.
I know nothing about it.	我一眼勿曉得	°Ngoo ih-ngan 'veh °hyau-tuh.
He knows.	伊曉得拉哉	Yi °hyau-tuh la° tse.
Now I know.	我曉得哩哉	°Ngoo °hyau-tuh li tse.
How did you find it out?	儂那曉得 儂那能曉得	Nong° °nang °hyau-tuh? Nong° na°-nung °hyau-tuh?
Why do I not know?	有啥勿曉得 為啥勿曉得	°Yeu sa° 'veh °hyau-tuh? We° sa° 'veh °hyau-tuh?
You ought to know.	儂應該曉得 儂該應曉得	Nong° iung-ke °hyau-tuh. Nong° ke-iung °hyau-tuh.
What do you know?	儂曉得个啥	Nong° °hyau-tuh kuh sa?
Difficult to know.	煩難曉得	Van-nan °hyau-tuh.
Easy enough to find out.	容易曉得	Yong-yi° °hyau-tuh.
(I) know it.	曉得哉	°Hyau-tuh tse.
You don't know.	儂勿曉得	Nong° 'veh °hyau-tuh.
I knew he would come to grief.	我曉得伊要碰着煩難	°Ngoo °hyau-tuh yi iau° bang°-dzak van-nan.
He has not yet known anything about it.	伊勿曾曉得	Yi 'veh-zung °hyau-tuh.
To understand; to comprehend.	懂	°Tong.

English	Chinese	Romanization
Do you understand?	懂否	°Tong va°?
I understand (or comprehend).	懂个 我懂个 懂个哉	°Tong kuh; °ngoo °tong kuh; °Tong kuh tse.
I do not understand.	勿懂 我勿懂	'Veh °tong; °ngoo 'veh °tong.
I am unable to understand.	我懂勿來	°Ngoo °tong 'veh le.
It is incomprehensible.	懂勿來个	°Tong 'veh le kuh.
I do not yet understand.	我勿曾懂	°Ngoo 'veh-zung °tong.
I don't comprehend anything about it.	一顏勿懂	Ih ngan 'veh °tong.
Now I understand.	懂哩哉	°Tong °li tse.
Can you comprehend it?	懂得出否	°Tong tuh ts'eh va°?
I can not understand it.	我懂勿出	°Ngoo °tong 'veh ts'eh.
To look; to see.	看	K'oen°.
I saw.	我看見个	°Ngoo k'oen°-kyien° kuh.
I have seen.	我看見哉	°Ngoo k'oen°-kyien° tse.
I had seen.	我已經看見哉	°Ngoo °i-kyung k'oen°-kyien° tse.
Look.	看看看	K'oen° k'oen° k'oen°.
I did not see.	我勿看見	°Ngoo 'veh k'oen°-kyien°.
Who saw it?	啥人看見	Sa° nyung k'oen°-kyien°?
Have you seen it? have you ever seen it?	看見歇否	K'oen°-kyien° hyih va°?
I have seen it; I have seen it before.	我看見歇个	°Ngoo k'oen°-kyien° hyih kuh.
I have not yet seen it.	我勿曾看見歇	°Ngoo 'veh-zung k'oen°-kyien° hyih.
I do not see it.	我勿看見	°Ngoo 'veh k'oen°-kyien°.

I can not see it.	我看勿見	°Ngoo k'oen° 'veh kyien°.
I can or do see it.	我看得見	°Ngoo k'oen° tuh kyien°.
Look at me; do as I do.	看我	K'oen° °ngoo.
I don't wish to see it.	我勿要看	°Ngoo 'veh iau° k'oen°.
Don't look at it.	勿要看	'Veh iau° k'oen°.
Disagreeable to behold.	難看	Nan k'oen°.
To look down upon.	看勿起	K'oen° 'veh °chi.
Not in accordance with one's fancy.	看勿中	K'oen° 'veh tsong°.
To inspect; to examine.	看看	K'oen° k'oen°.
To attend theatres.	看戲	K'oen° hyi°.
Pretty; handsome; fine, etc.	好看	°Hau k'oen°.
Not pretty, handsome, or fine, etc.	勿好看	'Veh °hau k'oen°.
How do you regard it?	儂看起來那能	Nong° k'oen° °chi le °na-nung?
I do not see distinctly.	我看勿清爽	°Ngoo k'oen° 'veh ts'ing-°saung.
I can see distinctly.	我看得清爽	°Ngoo k'oen° tuh ts'ing-°saung.
To forget.	忘記	Maung°-kyi°.
Did you forget? or have you forgotten?	忘記否	Maung° kyi° va°?
I have not forgotten.	我勿忘記	°Ngoo 'veh maung°-kyi°.
Do not forget.	勿要忘記	'Veh iau° maung°-kyi°.
I will not, or did not forget.	勿忘記个	'Veh maung°-kyi° kuh.
I forget it.	我忘記哉 忘記脫哉	°Ngoo maung°-kyi° tse; maung°-kyi°-t'eh tse.

English	Chinese	Romanization
A forgetful fellow.	忘記大	Maung°-kyi° doo°.
By no means forget.	忘記勿得 決決勿要忘記	Maung°-kyi° 'veh tuh. Kyoeh kyoeh 'veh iau° maung°-kyi°.
Remember.	記 記得	Kyi°; kyi°-tuh.
Do you remember?	記得否	Kyi°-tuh va°?
To look for.	尋	Zing.
To find.	尋着	Zing-dzak.
Look for it.	尋尋看	Zing zing k'oen°.
Go look for it.	去尋	Chi° zing.
Have you looked for it?	尋歇末	Zing hyih meh?
I have looked for it.	尋過歇個	Zing koo° hyih kuh.
Have you found it?	尋着末	Zing-dzak meh?
Did you find it?	尋着否	Zing-dzak va°?
I have found it.	尋着哉	Zing-dzak tse.
I found it.	尋着個	Zing-dzak kuh.
I can not, or could not find it.	尋勿着	Zing 'veh dzak.
I did not find it.	尋勿着個	Zing 'veh dzak kuh.
You must find it.	終要尋着個	Tsong iau° zing-dzak kuh.
I have not yet found it.	勿曾尋着	'Veh-zung zing-dzak.
Look everywhere.	各處尋	Kauh-ts'u° zing.
I have looked everywhere and can not find it.	各處尋到家尋勿着	Kauh-ts'u° zing tau°-ku, zing 'veh dzak.
If you do not find it, you must pay for it.	尋勿着末要儂賠個	Zing 'veh dzak meh, iau° nong° be kuh.
I have looked everywhere and can not find it.	尋來尋去尋勿着	Zing le zing chi°, zing 'veh dzak.

To listen; to hear.	聽	T'ing.
I hear.	我聽見	°Ngoo t'ing-kyien°.
I heard.	我聽見个	°Ngoo t'ing-kyien° kuh.
He did not hear.	伊勿聽見 伊勿聽得	Yi 'veh t'ing-kyien°; yi 'veh t'ing-tuh.
Listen; give attention.	聽拉	T'ing la°.
Do you hear distinctly (or understandingly)?	儂聽得出否	Nong° t'ing-tuh-ts'eh va°?
I hear (understandingly).	我聽得出	°Ngoo t'ing-tuh-ts'eh.
Listen to me.	聽我	T'ing °ngoo.
Listen.	聽聽看 聽拉看	T'ing t'ing k'oen°; t'ing la° k'oen°.
To eavesdrop.	聽壁脚	T'ing pih-kyak.
To listen to a discourse.	聽書	T'ing su.
To listen to singing.	聽唱	T'ing ts'aung°.
Pleasant to listen to.	好聽	°Hau t'ing.
Not pleasant to hear.	勿好聽	'Veh °hau t'ing.
Don't listen.	勿要聽	'Veh iau° t'ing.
I don't want to hear.	我勿要聽	°Ngoo 'veh iau° t'ing.
It should not be heard.	聽勿得个	T'ing 'veh tuh kuh.
I will follow your advice.	我聽儂 我聽儂个吩咐	°Ngoo t'ing nong°; °ngoo t'ing nong° kuh fung-foo°.
I have never heard it.	我勿曾聽見歇	°Ngoo 'veh-zung t'ing-kyien° hyih.
I have heard it before.	我聽過歇	°Ngoo t'ing koo° hyih.
I have not yet heard of it.	我勿曾聽見歇	°Ngoo 'veh-zung t'ing-kyien° hyih.
I have heard it reported.	我聽聞	°Ngoo t'ing vung.

Don't listen to rumors.	勿要聽謠言	'Veh iau° t'ing yau-yien.
I can't brook that.	我聽勿進	°Ngoo t'ing 'veh tsing°.
I do not hear distinctly.	我聽勿清爽	°Ngoo t'ing 'veh ts'ing-°saung.
I can hear very distinctly.	我聽得蠻清爽	°Ngoo t'ing tuh 'man ts'ing-°saung.
To think; to consider; to reflect.	想	°Siang.
Think about it; think awhile.	想想看	°Siang °siang k'oen°.
Can not call to mind.	想勿出	°Siang 'veh ts'eh.
Can call to mind.	想得出　想着	°Siang tuh ts'eh; °siang-dzak.
Consider the matter.	想起來看	°Siang °chi le k'oen°.
Think of me; remember me.	想着我	°Siang-dzak °ngoo.
Did not think of.	勿想着　想勿着	'Veh °siang-dzak; °siang 'veh dzak.
To think to no purpose.	白想脫	Bak °siang t'eh.
To consider fully; to think of every point.	想到家	°Siang tau°-ka.
Can not think of every point.	想勿到家	°Siang 'veh tau°-ka.
I think; in my opinion.	我想	°Ngoo °siang.
What do you think of it?	儂想那能　儂想起來那能	Nong° °siang °na-nung? Nong° °siang-°chi le °na-nung?
To think of; meditate upon.	想念	°Siang-nyan°.
To have designs upon.	想頭	°Siang-deu.
No designs, or expectations.	無想頭	M °siang-deu.

To believe.	信　相信	Sing°; °siang-sing°.
I do not believe it.	我勿相信	°Ngoo 'veh siang-sing°.
Do you believe it?	儂相信否	Nony° siang sing° va°?
I believe it.	我相信个	°Ngoo siang-sing° kuh.
I have confidence in him.	我相信伊	°Ngoo siang-sing° yi.
I have no confidence in him.	我勿相信伊	°Ngoo 'veh siang-sing° yi.
It is difficult to believe.	煩難相信	Van-nan siang-sing°.
It is impossible not to believe it.	勿得勿相信	'Veh tuh 'veh siang-sing°.
To believe in Buddhist idols.	信佛	Sing° veh.
Buddha.	佛	Veh.
To believe in Jesus.	信耶穌　相信耶穌	Sing° Ya-soo; siang-sing°· Ya-soo.
To worship, or believe in no God.	百勿相信　百勿信	Pak 'veh siang-sing°; Pak 'veh sing°.
Faith; trust.	信托	Sing°-t'auh.
Don't believe it.	勿要相信	'Veh iau° siang-sing°.
It won't do to take his word.	勿好相信伊	'Veh °hau siang-sing° yi.
To delight in.	相信	Siang-sing°.
He delights in wine.	伊相信酒	Yi siang-sing° °tsieu.
To strike; to chastise; to fight.	打	°Tang.
He struck me.	伊打我	Yi °tang °ngoo.
They are fighting.	垃拉相打	Leh-la° siang-°tang.
Able to whip.	打得過	°Tang tuh koo°.
Not able to whip.	打勿過	°Tang 'veh koo°.

To fight a battle.	打仗	°Tang-tsang°.
To deliver a general charge.	攻打	Kong-°tang.
To gain a victory.	打贏　打勝仗	°Tang-ying; °tang sung°-tsang°.
To lose a battle.	打輸　打敗　打敗仗	°Tang su; °tang ba°; °tang ba°-tsang°.
To shoot game.	打鴛	°Tang °tiau.
To shoot large game.	打獵	°Tang lih.
To hit.	打着	°Tang dzak.
To miss.	打勿着	°Tang 'veh dzak.
To wound.	打傷	°Tang saung.
To ring, or strike a large bell.	打鐘	°Tang tsong.
To thrash wheat.	打麥	°Tang mak.
To thrash rice.	打稻	°Tang °dau.
To drive piles.	打樁	°Tang tsaung.
To make inquiries.	打聽　打緝	°Tang t'ing°; °Tang ts'ih.
To make a bamboo fence.	打笆	°Tang po.
To build a cooking range.	打竈頭	°Tang tsau°-deu.
To make (any instrument of metal).	打	°Tang.
To make a sword, or knife.	打刀	°Tang tau.
To draw a plan.	打槀子	°Tang °kau-°tsz.
To prosecute at law.	打官司	°Tang kwen-sz.
To speak in Mandarin.	打官話	°Tang kwen-wo°.

To slap one in the face.	打耳光	°T'ang nyi°-kwaung.
To dress in a showy manner.	打扮	°T'ang-pan°.
Foolish and impudent talking.	打棚	°T'ang-bang.
To strike fire.	打火	°T'ang °hoo.
To kill.	打殺	°T'ang sah.
To injure by striking.	打壞　打傷	°T'ang wa°; °t'ang saung.
To rap; to knock.	敲	K'au.
Knock at the door.	敲門	K'au mung.
To drive a nail.	敲釘	K'au ting.
To break in pieces.	敲碎	K'au se°.
To beat flat.	敲扁	K'au °pien.
Knock it off.	敲脫	K'au t'eh.
To pound.	敲	K'au.
To cut (*as with a small knife*).	割	Koeh.
To inflict a wound by cutting.	割傷	Koeh-saung.
Cut it open.	割開　割開來	Koeh-k'e; koeh-k'e-le.
Cut it in two.	割斷	Koeh-°doen.
Cut it off.	割脫	Koeh-t'eh.
To cut (*as with sword, heavy knife, or ax*).	斬	Tsan.
To wound, as with a sword or ax.	斬傷	Tsan saung.
Cut it in two.	斬斷	Tsan °doen.
Cut it off.	斬脫	Tsan t'eh.
To split.	劈	P'ih.

Split it open.	劈開來　劈開	P'ih k'e le; p'ih k'e.
Can not split it.	劈勿開	P'ih 'veh k'e.
To split wood.	劈柴	P'ih za.
To split off.	劈脫	P'ih-t'eh.
To saw.	截　鋸	Zih; ka°.
Saw it off.	截脫　鋸脫	Zih-t'eh; ka°-t'eh.
Saw it in two.	截斷　鋸斷	Zih-°doen; ka°-°doen.
Saw it open.	截開來　鋸開來	Zih k'e le; ka° k'e le.
Too hard to be sawn.	截勿落　鋸勿落	Zih 'veh lauh; k'a° 'veh lauh.
To sweep.	掃	°Sau.
Sweep the floor.	掃地　掃掃地	°Sau di°; °sau °sau di°.
Sweep it up.	掃脫	°Sau t'eh.
Sweep clean.	掃葛瀝　掃乾淨	°Sau koch-lih; °sau koen-zing°.
To kill; to decapitate; to butcher.	殺	Sah.
To execute a man.	殺人　殺頭	Sah nyung; sah deu.
To butcher a beef.	殺牛	Sah nyeu.
To kill a fowl.	殺鷄	Sah kyi.
To butcher a sheep.	殺羊	Sah yang.
A slaughter house.	殺牛場	Sah nyeu dzang.
To wage war.	相殺	Siang sah.
To gain a victory.	殺贏	Sah yung.
To lose a battle.	殺敗	Sah ba°.
To write.	寫　寫字	°Sia; °sia z°.

Write a letter.	寫一封信　寫信	°Sia ih fong sing° ; °sia sing°.
Have you written a letter?	信寫末	Sing° °sia meh ?
I have written.	信寫拉哉	Sing° °sia la° tse.
To make a record (in an account book).	寫帳　上帳	°Sia tsang° ; °zaung tsang°.
Can you write?	字會寫否	Z° 'we° °sia va° ?
I can not write.	寫勿來	°Sia 'veh le.
He can write.	伊會寫　伊寫得來	Yi 'we° °sia ; yi °sia tuh le.
Write it distinctly.	字寫來清爽	Z° °sia le ts'ing-°saung.
Badly written.	字寫得勿好	Z° °sia tuh 'veh °hau.
To boil.	煠	Zah.
Boil a few eggs.	煠兩个蛋	Zah °liang kuh dan°.
I don't want them too hard.	勿要忒硬	'Veh iau° t'uh ngang°.
To grill; to broil.	燻	Hyuin.
Grilled fowl.	燻鷄	Hyuin kyi.
Broiled steak.	燻牛肉	Hyuin nyeu nyok.
Broil it rare.	要燻來生	Iau hyuin le sang.
Broil it well done.	要燻來熟	Iau hyuin le zok.
To bake; to roast; to warm one's self.	烘	Hong.
To wash.	淨	Zing°.
Wash your hands.	淨手	Zing° °seu.
To wash one's feet.	淨脚	Zing° kyak.
To bathe.	淨浴	Zing° yok.
To wash clothes.	淨衣裳	Zing° i-zaung.

Wash clean.	淨乾淨	Zing° koen-zing.°
Can not wash it out.	淨勿脫	Zing° 'veh t'eh.
To wipe.	揩	K'a.
Wipe or wash the face.	揩面	K'a mien°.
Wipe it off.	揩脫	K'a-t'eh.
Wipe it.	揩揩	K'a k'a.
Wipe clean.	揩乾淨	K'a koen-zing°.
Wipe the table.	揩檯子	K'a de-°tsz.
Wipe clean the knives, forks, etc.	刀义咾啥揩乾淨	Tau ts'o lau sa° k'a° koen-zing.
Wipe clean the plates, cups, etc.	盆子杯子咾啥揩乾淨	Bung-°tsz pe-°tsz lau sa° k'a koen-zing°.
Can not wipe it off.	揩勿脫 揩勿落	K'a 'veh t'eh; k'a 'veh lauh.
Wipe it again.	再揩	tse° k'a.
Wipe it till it is clean.	揩直到乾淨	K'a dzuh-tau° koen-zing°.
Have you wiped it?	揩歇末	K'a hyih meh?
I have wiped it.	揩拉哉 揩歇個	K'a la° tse; k'a hyih kuh.
You have not wiped it clean.	揩得勿乾淨	K'a tuh 'veh koen-zing°.
I want you to wipe it cleaner.	要揩來乾淨點	Iau° k'a le koen-zing° tien.
I want you to wipe every day.	要儂日多揩揩	Iau° nong° nyih-too k'a k'a.
To sew; to stitch.	紉	Ling.
Take a stitch.	紉一針 紉兩針	Ling ih tsung; ling °liang tsung.

To make clothes.	紉衣裳	Ling i-zaung.
To iron; to burn, or scald.	盪	T'aung°.
To cut, or engrave.	刻	K'uh.
To cut characters.	刻字	K'uh z°.
To engrave.	刻花	K'uh hwo.
To stereotype.	刻板子	K'uh °pan-°tsz.
To cut a stamp.	刻印子	K'uh iung°-°tsz.
To light a fire.	生火	Sang °hoo.
You have lighted it badly.	儂生來勿好	Nong° sang le 'veh °hau.
Light it again.	再生	Tse° sang.
To light a lamp, or candle.	點燈	°Tien tung.
To light a fire (or lamp)	點火	°Tien °hoo.
It will not light.	點勿上	°Tien 'veh °zzung.
To take.	担	Tan.
Take it; take it away.	担去	Tan chi°.
Bring it here; bring to me.	担來	Tan le.
Unable to take or carry it.	担勿動 担勿起	Tan 'veh °dong; tan 'veh °chi.
Who took it?	啥人担	Sa°-nyung tan?
He took it.	伊担个	Yi tan kuh.
Did any one see him take it?	有啥人看見伊担否	°Yeu sa° nyung k'oen°-kyien° yi tan va°?
I saw him, with my own eyes, take it away.	我親眼看見伊担去	°Ngoo ts'ing °ngan k'oen°-kyien° yi tan chi°.

English	Chinese	Romanization
Where are you going with that?	第个儂担到那裏去	°Di-kuh nong° tan tau° °'a°-°li chi°?
Take it out.	担出去	Tan ts'eh chi°.
Take it inside.	担到裏向去	Tan tau° °li-hyang° chi°.
Take it and throw it away.	担去甩脫	Tan chi° hwah-t'eh.
I did not take it.	我勿担个	°Ngoo 'veh tan kuh.
Take it above stairs.	担到樓上去	Tan tau° leu laung° chi°.
Take it on board ship.	担到船上去	Tan tau° zen laung° chi°.
To ascend; to descend; to get up.	踩	Lok.
Get up.	踩起來	Lok-°chi-le.
Come up.	踩上來	Lok-°zaung°-le.
Go up; mount; ascend.	踩上去	Lok-°zaung-°chi.
Come down; descend.	踩下來	Lok-°'au-le.
Go down.	踩下去	Lok-°'au-chi°.
Can not go up, or mount.	踩勿上	Lok 'veh °zaung.
Can not get up (for want of strength)	踩勿起	Lok 'veh °chi.
Able to get up.	踩得起	Lok tuh °chi.
To ride on horse back.	騎馬	Ji °mo.
To catch; to seize; to arrest.	捉	Tsauh.
Catch him.	捉伊	Tsauh yi.
Catch thief.	捉賊	Tsauh zuh.
To arrest a man.	捉人	Tsauh nyung.
Unable to catch, or arrest.	捉勿着	Tsauh 'veh dzak.

Able to catch, etc.	捉得着	Tsauh tuh dzak.
To arrest gamblers.	捉賭	Tsauh °too.
Not sufficient force (or skill) to catch, or arrest.	捉勿住	Tsauh 'veh dzu°.
I have caught him.	捉着哉	Tsauh dzɪk tse.
To make a dam.	築壩	Tsauh po°.
To make a grave mound.	築坟山	Tsauh vung-san.
To reap wheat.	斫麥	Tsauh mak.
To cut rice.	斫稻	Tsauh °dau.
To cut grass.	斫草	Tsauh °ts'au.
To brush.	刷	Seh.
To brush shoes.	刷鞋子	Seh 'a-°tsz.
To brush clothes.	刷衣裳	Seh i-zaung.
To fear; dread.	怕	P'o°.
Do you fear?	怕否	P'o° va°?
I do fear.	我怕个	°Ngoo p'o° kuh.
What do you fear?	怕啥	P'o° sa°?
I do not fear.	我勿怕	°Nyoo 'veh p'o°.
Don't fear.	勿要怕	'Veh iau° p'o°.
There is nothing to fear.	無啥怕	M sa° p'o°.
I am apprehensive he will not come.	只怕伊勿來	Tsuh-p'o° yi 'veh le.
I fear you will lose money by it.	恐怕要蝕本	°K'ong-p'o° iau° zeh °puny.
I fear it will not succeed.	恐怕勿成功	°K'ong-p'o° 'veh dzung-kong.
To fear death.	怕死	P'o° °si.
To provide.	預備	Yui-be°.

Make good preparation.	預備好	Yui-be° °hau.
Have you got everything ready?	預備好末	Yui-be° °hau meh?
I have everything ready.	預備好拉哉	Yui-be° °hau la° tse.
He has not provided a thing.	一樣勿曾預備	Ih yang 'veh zung yui-be°.
To move.	動	°Dong.
Don't move.	勿要動	'Veh iau° °dong.
Don't touch it; don't have anything to do with the matter.	勿要動 動勿得个	'Veh iau° °dong; °dong 'veh tuh kuh.
It is loose, or unstable.	搖動哉 動咾動	Yau-°dong tse; °dong lau °dong.
Steady, immovable.	動也勿動	°Dong °a 'veh °dong.
To start; to embark.	動身	°Dong-sung.
To commence work.	動手	°Dong °seu.
It does not move in the least.	一眼勿動	Ih ngan 'veh °dong.
To dig (*as with a pick*).	垄	Bung°.
To dig up loosely.	垄鬆	Bung° song.
To dig up a garden.	垄園地	Bung° yoen-di°.
Too hard to dig.	垄勿落	Bung° 'veh lauh.
Dig it deep.	垄來深	Bung° le sung.
Dig it deeper.	垄來深點	Bung° le sung tien.
To plant.	種	Tsong°.
To cultivate a farm.	種田	Tsong° dien.
To cultivate a garden.	種園地	Tsong° yoen-di°.
What are you planting?	儂拉種啥	Nong° la tsong° sa°?

English	Chinese	Romanization
I am planting vegetables.	種菜	Tsong° ts'e°.
To plant flowers.	種花草	Tsong° hwo-°ts'au.
Plant them well.	種來好	Tsong° le °hau.
Plant them deep.	種來深	Tsong° le sung.
To sow, or do that from which one may expect evil fruit.	種禍殃根	Tsong° 'oo°-iang-kung.
Have you finished planting?	種完末	Tsong° wen mch?
I have finished.	種完哉	Tsong° wen tsc.
To dwell.	住	Dzu°.
Where do you live?	儂住拉那裏	Nong° dzu° la° °'a-°li?
I live in the city.	我住拉城裏	°Ngoo dzu° la° dzung °li.
I live outside of the city.	我住拉城外	°Ngoo dzu° la° dzung nga°.
Can not dwell in so small a place.	住勿落	Dzu° 'vch lauh.
To give birth to; to rear.	養	°Yang.
To beg.	討	°T'au.
To beg for food.	討飯	°T'au van°.
To dun.	討帳	°T'au tsang°.
To dun for a debt of long standing.	討債	°T'au tsa°.
To get married.	討娘子	°T'au nyang-°tsz.
To beg for something in addition to what is due.	討饒	°T'au nyau.
To annoy.	討厭	°T'au ien°.
To command.	吩咐	Fung-foo°.

Who gave the order?	啥人吩咐	$Sa^°$ nyung fung-foo°?
To bind with a cord.	綁	°Paung.
Tie him to a tree.	綁拉樹上	°Paung la° zu° laung°.
To tie a man hands and feet.	綑綁	°Kw'ung °paung.
To tie (*as a small parcel*).	紮	Tsah.
Tie it well.	紮好	Tsah °hau.
To bite; to bark.	咬	°Ngau.
Will that dog bite?	第隻狗要咬个否	°Di tsak °keu iau° °ngau k'ih va°?
He will bite.	要咬个	Iau° °ngau kuh.
He will not bite.	勿咬　勿咬个	'Veh °ngau; 'veh °ngau kuh.
Did you hear the dog bark last night?	昨夜頭狗咬聽見否	Zo ya°-deu °keu °ngau t'ing-kyien° va°?
To blow.	吹	Ts'z.
Blow it out (*as a light*).	吹隱	Ts'z °iung.
Can not blow it out.	吹勿隱	Ts'z 'veh °iung.
To blow into a blaze.	吹旺	Ts'z yaung°.
Can not blow into a blaze.	吹勿旺	Ts'z 'veh yaung°.
Can be blown into a blaze.	吹得旺	Ts'z tuh yaung°.
Blow it off.	吹脫	Ts'z t'eh.
Can not blow it off.	吹勿脫	Ts'z 'veh t'eh.
The wind blew it off.	風吹脫个	Fong ts'z t'eh kuh.
To blow a trumpet.	吹招軍	Ts'z tsau-kyuin.
To play the clarion.	吹喇叭	Ts'z la°-pa.

English	Chinese	Romanization
To play the flute.	吹笛	Ts'z dih.
Can not play.	吹勿來	Ts'z 'veh le.
Try and blow it.	吹吹看	Ts'z ts'z k'oen°.
To learn.	學	'Auh.
To learn business.	學生意	'Auh sang-i°.
To learn to write.	學寫字	'Auh °sia z°.
To learn the Shanghai dialect.	學上海話	'Auh Zaung°-°he wo°.
To learn Mandarin.	學官話	'Auh Kwen-wo°.
To learn the classic style.	學文理	'Auh vung-°li.
Difficult to learn.	難學个	Nan 'auh kuh.
No inclination to learn.	無心相學	M sing °siang 'auh.
Just commenced to learn.	纔學	K'an 'auh.
Been learning a long time.	學之長遠哉	'Auh tsz dzang-°yoen ´tse.
To succeed in learning.	學成功	'Auh dzung-kong.
Did not (or will not) succeed in learning.	學勿成功	'Auh 'veh dzung-kong.
A school room.	學堂	'Auh-daung.
A pupil.	學生子	'Auh-sang-°tsz.
Can not learn.	學勿來	'Auh 'veh le.
Can learn.	學得來	'Auh tuh le.
Confucian temple.	學宮	'Auh kong.
The teacher of graduates.	學老師	'Auh-°lau-sz.
To aspire to a high degree of virtue; to reform.	學好	'Auh °hau.

To learn bad habits.	學獠	'Auh °liau.
To break (as a piece of timber or cord.)	斷	°Doen.
It is broken (in two).	斷哉	°Doen tse.
To break with the hands (as a stick).	灣斷	'Wan-°doen.
It can not be broken.	灣勿斷	'Wan 'veh °doen.
To fall.	跌	Tih.
He had a fall.	伊跌之一交	Yi tih tsz° ih kau.
He or it fell down.	跌下來	Tih °·au le.
It fell down of itself.	自家跌下來	Z-°ka tih °·au le.
Be careful or you will fall.	當心要跌个	Taung-sing iau° tih kuh.
The price has fallen.	價錢跌哉	Ka°-dien tih tse.
How much has it fallen?	跌之幾化	Tih-tsz° °kyi-hau°?
The price will fall.	價錢要跌个	Ka°-dien iau° tih kuh.
Let it fall.	讓伊跌末哉	Nyang° yi tih mch tse.
It is not likely to fall very much.	勿見得跌啥幾化	'Veh kien° tuh tih sa° °kyi-hau°.
He fell in the river or canal.	跌拉河裏	Tih la° ʻoo-°li.
Wounded by a fall.	跌傷　跌獠	Tih saung; Tih °liau.
To rise (as tide, etc.)	漲	°Tsang.
The price will rise.	價錢要漲	Ka°-dien iau° °tsang.
The price has risen.	價錢漲哉	Ka°-dien °tsang tse.
The rising tide.	漲水漲潮	Tsang° °sz; tsang° dzau.
The flood tide has made.	水漲哉　潮漲哉　潮來哉	°Sz tsang° tse; dzau tsang° tse; dzau le tse.

English	Chinese	Romanization
The tide ceases to rise.	潮漲停哉 平水哉	Dzau tsang° ding tse; bing °sz tse.
Has the flood tide made?	潮漲末 潮來末 水漲末	Dzu tsang° meh; dzau le meh; °sz tsang° meh?
The flood tide has not yet made.	潮勿曾漲 潮勿曾來	Dzau 'veh zung tsang; dzau 'veh zung le.
To fall (*as the tide*).	落	Lauh.
The falling or ebb tide.	落潮 落水	Lauh dzau; lauh °sz.
The tide is falling.	潮落哉	Dzau lauh tse.
The tide ceases to fall.	潮落停哉 潮落過哉	Dzau lauh ding tse; dzau lauh koo° tse.
To choose; to select.	揀 揀選	°Kan; °kan-°sien.
Select good ones.	揀好个	°Kan °hau kuh.
Select cheap ones.	揀强个	°Kan jang kuh.
Select the most available.	揀便宜个	°Kan bien-nyi kuh.
Choose for yourself.	聽揀	T'ing° °kan.
Pick out.	揀出來	°Kan ts'eh le.
Can not make a selection.	揀勿出	°Kan 'veh ts'eh.
To pick over tea.	揀茶葉	°Kan dzo-yih.
That which is left after making a selection.	揀剩拉个 揀賸拉个	°Kan dzang° la° kuh; °Kan° dzung° la° kuh.
To stick, or adhere.	搥 搥住 搥牢	Teh; teh dzu°; teh lau.
Will not stick, or adhere.	搥勿住 搥勿牢	Teh 'veh dzu°; teh 'veh lau.
To throw (*as a stone*).	搥	Teh.

To flee; to run away.	逃走	Dau-°tseu.
He has escaped.	逃走哉	Dau-°tseu tse.
He will run away.	伊要逃走	Yi iau° dau-°tseu.
Where has he escaped to?	逃走到那裏去	Dau-°tseu tau° °'a-°li chi°?
He can not escape.	逃走勿脫	Dau-°tseu 'veh t'eh.
To fly.	飛	Fi.
It has flown.	飛哉 飛之去哉	Fi tse`; Fi tsz chi° tse.
It will fly.	要飛个	Iau° fi kuh.
It can not fly.	伊勿會飛 飛勿動	Yi 'veh 'we° fi; fi 'veh °dong.
To fly up.	飛上去	Fi zaung° chi°.
To fly about.	飛來飛去	Fi le fi chi°.
The feathered tribe.	飛禽	Fi-jung.
Birds and animals.	飛禽走獸	Fi-jung °tseu-seu°.
To forsake; to desert; to depart from, etc.	離開	Li-k'e.
He forsook me.	伊離開之我	Yi li-k'e-tsz °ngoo.
Don't forsake me.	勿要離開我	'Veh iau° li-k'e °ngoo.
From the time he left home till now.	離開之屋裡到難	Li-k'e-tsz° ok-°li tau° nan.
He has forsaken me.	伊離開之我哉	Yi li-k'e-tsz °ngoo tse.
To hang; to suspend.	掛	Kwo°.
Hang it up.	掛拉 掛起來	Kwo°-la°; kwo° °chi le.
It is hanging up.	掛起拉	Kwo° °chi la°.
Nowhere to hang it.	無掛處	M kwo°-ts'u°.

To make a display of lanterns; to illuminate.	掛燈	Kwo° tung.
To carry a load (*as one man with a load suspended on the two ends of a stick*).	挑	T'iau.
To carry a load (*as a load suspended between two men, on a bamboo*).	扛	Kaung.
One man can not carry so heavy a load; it will require two men.	一个人挑勿起要扛个	Ih kuh nyung t'iau 'veh °chi, iau° kaung kuh.
To carry a load on the back.	背	Pe°.
To carry a load on the shoulder.	掮	Jien.
To carry a load in one hand (*as a bucket*).	拎	Ling.
Take it with you.	帶去	Ta° chi°.
Bring it with you.	帶來	Ta° le.
To begin; to commence; the commencement.	起 起頭 開場	°Chi; °Chi-deu; k'e-dzang.
When will you commence?	幾時開場	°Kyi-z k'e-dzang?
When will you commence (as an engagement)?	幾時做起	°Kyi-z tsoo° °chi?
When shall it commence (as interest or rent)?	幾時起	°Kyi-z °chi?
When did you begin (as an engagement)?	幾時做起个	°Kyi-z tsoo° °chi kuh?

English	Chinese	Romanization
To repair.	脩　收築	Sieu; seu-tsauh.
Take it and mend it.	担去收築	Tan chi° seu-tsauh.
Repairs.	脩理	Sieu-°li.
To reform.	脩身　脩心	Sieu sung; sieu sing.
To take hold.	揑	Nyah.
Take hold of it.	揑拉	Nyah la°.
Hold fast.	揑住　揑好	Nyah dzu°; nyah °hau.
Take it in your hand.	揑拉手裏	Nyah la° °seu °li.
Can not hold it.	揑勿住	Nyah 'veh dzu°.
To have charge of an affair, or a work; to exercise authority; also the handle of anything.	揑手	Nyah °seu.
No means of taking hold of it.	無揑手	M nyah °seu.
To crush in the hand.	揑碎	Nyah se°.
To let go; to put down; to discharge a gun; to liberate.	放	Faung°.
Let go.	放手	Faung° °seu.
Put it down.	放下來　放拉	Faung° °au le; faung° la°.
Let him go.	放伊去	Faung° yi chi°.
To set at liberty.	放脫	Faung° t'eh.
Put it on the table.	放拉檯子上	Faung° la° de-°tsz laung°.
To place money at interest.	放債	Faung° tsa°.
To sell on credit.	放帳	Faung° tsang°.
We do not sell on credit.	伲勿放帳	Nyi° 'veh faung° tsang°.

To dismiss a school.	放學	Faung° 'auh.
To commit an incendiary.	放火	Faung° °hoo.
To discharge a cannon.	放砲	Faung° p'au°.
To fire crackers.	放砲仗	Faung° p'au°-dzing°.
To bleed.	放血	Faung° hyoeh.
To fly a kite.	放鷂子	Faung° yau-°tsz.
Quiet your mind; have no apprehension.	放心	Faung°-sing.
I can not suppress my anxiety.	我勿能彀放心	°Ngoo 'veh nung-keu° faung°-sing.
Put it in the drawer.	放拉抽屉裡	Faung° la° ts'eu-t'i li.
Put them down in one place.	放拉一塊	Faung° la° ih kw'e°.
He has been set at liberty.	放脫哉	Faung° t'eh tse.
To hide; to conceal.	囥　囥攏	K'aung°; k'aung°-°long.
Hide it.	囥攏	K'aung°-°long.
It is concealed.	囥攏拉	K'aung°-°long la°.
No place to conceal it.	無囥處	M k'aung° ts'u°.
It can not be concealed.	囥勿攏	K'aung° 'veh °long.
Concealed on his person.	囥拉身邊	K'aung° la° sung-pien.
Don't conceal it.	勿耍囥攏	'Veh iau° k'aung°-°long.
Where have you concealed it?	囥拉那裏	K'aung° la° °'a-le° ?
I have not concealed it.	我勿囥攏	°Ngoo 'veh k'aung°-°long.
To open; to commence.	開	K'e.
Open the door.	開門	K'e mung.
Can not open it.	開勿來	K'e 'veh le.

Must not be opened.	勿好開	'Veh °hau k'e.
It may be opened.	好開个	°Hau k'e kuh.
I can open it.	我開得來	°Ngoo k'e tuh le.
To open a box.	開箱子	K'e siang-°tsz.
Open the way.	開路	K'e loo°.
Not enough to meet expenses.	勿殼事開銷	'Veh keu° z° k'e siau.
To take anchor and set sail.	開船	K'e zen.
To commence speaking; to open the mouth.	開口	K'e °k'eu.
To enlighten.	開道	K'e dau°.
To open a firm.	開行	K'e 'aung.
To open a shop.	開店	K'e tien°.
Not yet opened.	勿曾開	'Veh-zung k'e.
It is open.	開拉哉	K'e la° tse.
To commence business.	開市　開張	K'e °z; k'e tsang.
To open a canal, etc.	開河	K'e 'oo.
To bloom.	開花	K'e hwo.
To scatter; to separate.	散開	San°-k'e.
To fire a cannon.	開砲	K'e p'au°.
Don't make it public.	勿要話開	'Veh iau° wo° k'e.
To commence speaking.	開講	K'e °kaung.
To shut; to close.	關	Kwan.
Shut the door, or gate.	關門	Kwan mung.
Shut it well.	關好	Kwan °hau.
Shut the window.	關窗	Kwan ts'aung.
Shut up.	關攏　關沒	Kwan °long; kwan meh.

English	Chinese	Romanization
It is shut.	關拉哉　關哉	Kwan la° tse; kwan tse.
Shut him out.	關出伊	Kwan ts'eh yi.
Shut him in.	關沒伊	Kwan meh yi.
To shut up shop.	關店	Kwan tien°.
That shop is closed.	第爿店關脫哉	°Di ban tien° kwan t'eh tse.
This door will not shut.	第扇門關勿上	°Di sen° mung kwan 'veh °zaung.
A custom house.	關	Kwan.
The custom house in Shanghai.	新關	Sing kwan.
A custom pass, or barrier.	關口	Kwan °k'eu.
Customs; duties.	關稅	Kwan soe°.
To evade the duties; to smuggle.	飛關　偷稅	Fi kwan; t'eu soe°.
To concern one.	關着	Kwan dzak.
It concerns you.	關着儂	Kwan dzak nong°.
It concerns me.	關着我	Kwan dzak °ngoo.
Does not concern.	勿關	'Veh kwan.
It does not concern me.	我勿關　勿關我　勿關我啥事	°Ngoo 'veh kwan; 'veh kwan °ngoo; 'veh kwan °ngoo sa° z°.
To be in great straits, or peril.	性命交關	Sing°-ming° kyau-kwan.
Give attention to for me; also notify.	關切	Kwan-ts'ih.
Send me a message; let me know.	關照我　關切我	Kwan-tsau° °ngoo; kwan-ts'ih °ngoo.
The god of war.	關帝　關老爺	Kwan-ti°; °Kwan °Lau-ya.

To put; to place.	擺	°Pa.
Place it securely.	擺好	°Pa °hau.
Place it level.	擺平	°Pa bing.
Place even and in order.	擺端正	°Pa toen-tsung°.
Can not place it level.	擺勿平	°Pa 'veh bing.
Put it above.	擺拉上頭	°Pa la° zaung°-deu.
Put it below.	擺拉下底	°Pa la° °'au-°ti.
Put it on the table.	擺拉檯子上	°Pa la° de-°tsz laung°.
Put it inside.	擺拉裡向	°Pa la° °li-hyang°.
Put it outside.	擺拉外頭	°Pa la° nga°-deu.
Put it in the chest.	擺拉箱子裡	°Pa la° siang-°tsz °li.
To decorate; the decorations of a room.	擺設	°Pa-seh.
A ferry boat.	擺渡船	°Pa-doo° zen.
To set, *or* lay the table.	擺檯子	°Pa de-°tsz.
To contribute; to tax; *also* a tax.	捐	Kyoen.
House tax.	房捐	Vaung-kyoen.
Taxes.	捐厘	Kyoen-li.
Impost tax.	厘捐	Li-kyoen.
Quarterly tax.	四季捐	Sz°-kyi° kyoen.
Monthly tax.	月捐	Nyoeh kyoen.
To borrow, *or* to lend.	借	Tsia°.
To borrow money.	借銀子	Tsia° nyung-°tsz.
Lend it to me.	借拉我	Tsia° la °ngoo.
Can not borrow.	借勿動	Tsia° 'veh-°dong.
I will not lend.	勿借	'Veh tsia°.
It is borrowed.	借拉个	Tsia° la° kuh.

English	Chinese	Romanization
It is loaned out.	借出去拉	Tsia° ts'eh chi° la°.
Sub-let.	轉借	°Tsen tsia°.
Can you borrow it?	好借否	°Hau tsia° va°?
Don't borrow.	勿要借	'Veh iau° tsia°.
To conduct; to guide.	領	°Ling.
Bring him in.	領進來	°Ling tsing°-le.
Conduct him out.	領出去	°Ling ts'eh-chi°.
The leader, the head man.	領頭人	°Ling-deu nyung.
The blind leading the blind.	瞎子領瞎子	Hah-°tsz °ling hah-°tsz.
A pilot.	領港个	°Ling °kaung kuh.
A pilot boat.	領港船	°Ling-°kaung-zen.
To nurse; to take charge of a child.	領小团	°Ling °siau-noen.
A collar.	一條領	Ih diau °ling.
To conduct out of the way.	領差	°Ling ts'o.
To lead (*as an animal*).	牽	Chien.
To lead a horse.	牽馬	Chien °mo.
Lead him in.	牽進來	Chien tsing° le.
Lead him out.	牽出去	Chien ts'eh chi°.
To lead by the hand (as a child).	牽手	Chien °seu.
To lose.	失脫　落脫	Seh-t'eh; lauh-t'eh.
I have lost it.	失脫哉　落脫哉	Seh-t'eh tse; lauh t'eh tse.
How much did you lose?	失脫幾化	Seh-t'eh °kyi-hau°?

English	Chinese	Romanization
He has lost all his capital.	本錢一齊失脫哉	°Pung-dien ih zi seh-t'eh tse.
I have lost heavily.	失脫之多化	Seh-t'eh-tsz too-hau°.
He can't afford to lose.	伊蝕勿起	Yi zeh 'veh °chi.
To meet; to come in contact with; to hit.	挷着　挷頭	Bang°-dzak; bang°-deu.
Did you meet him?	挷着否	Bang°-dzak va°?
Did not meet (or see).	挷勿着	Bang° 'veh-dzak.
I met him.	挷着个	Bang°-dzak kuh.
To butt (as a sheep or goat).	挷　撞	Bang°; Dzaung°.
To receive, or accept.	受	°Zeu.
To receive presents.	受禮物	°Zeu °li-'veh.
To receive an honor.	受賞賜	°Zeu °saung-sz°.
To suffer.	受苦　受難	°Zeu °k'oo; °zeu nan°.
To be imposed upon.	受黃	°Zeu waung.
To be put to the blush.	受無趣	°Zeu m-ts'ui°.
To decline (a favor).	勿受	'Veh °zeu.
To hand; to deliver in person.	授	Dzeu°.
Hand it to me.	授拉我	Dzeu° la° °ngoo.
Can not reach.	授勿着	Dzeu° 'veh dzak.
Hand it to him.	授拉伊	Dzeu° la° yi.
I delivered it to him.	我授拉伊	°Ngoo dzeu° la° yi.
To read.	讀　讀書　看書	Dok; dok su; k'oen° su.
He can not read.	讀勿來	Dok 'veh le.
A scholar; a literary man.	讀書人	Dok-su-nyung.

English	Chinese	Romanization
To rot.	爛	Lan.°
It is unsound.	爛哉	Lan° tse.
It is not rotten.	勿爛	'Veh lan.°
Mud.	爛泥	Lan°-nyi.
Muddy under foot.	地上爛	Di° laung° lan°.
Very muddy.	爛來死	Lan °le °si.
To walk.	走 跑	Tseu°; pau°.
Come here.	走來 跑來	Tseu° le; pau° le.
Walk faster.	走來快點 快點走	Tseu° le kw'a°-tien; kw'a°-tien °tseu.
Unable to walk.	走勿動 跑勿動	Tseu° 'veh °dong; pau° 'veh °dong.
I walked.	我走个 我跑來个	°Ngoo °tseu kuh; °ngoo pau° le kuh.
To run.	跑	Bau.
To run a horse-race.	跑馬	Bau °mo.
To count.	數	°Soo.
Count and see how many (or much).	數數看	°Soo °soo k'oen.°
Unable to count.	數勿出	Soo° 'veh ts'eh.
I have already counted.	數過歇哉	°Soo koo° hyih tse.
To deposit with another.	寄	Kyi.°
Deposit with me.	寄拉我	Kyi° la° °ngoo.
To send a letter or message.	寄信	Kyi° sing.°
To shave.	剃	T'i.°
To shave the beard.	剃鬚	T'i° soo.
To shave the head.	剃頭	T'i° deu.

To sink (*in water*).	沉	Dzung.
It will sink.	要沉个 要沉下去个	Iau° dzung kuh; iau° dzung °au ch'i° kuh.
To drown.	沉殺	Dzung sah.
To spin.	紡紗	°Faung-so.
To weave.	織布	Tsuh poo.°
To spread out; spread it out.	攤開來	T'an k'e le.
To steal.	偷　偷物事	T'eu; t'eu meh-zz.°
Secretly.	偷件子	T'eu-ben°-°tsz
To roll up.	捲攏	°Kyoen-°long.
To inform against.	狀覆	Zaung°-fok.
To institute a suit at law.	告狀	Kau°-zaung.°
To inform.	告訴　關照	Kau°-soo°; kwan-tsau.°
To swear.	罰咒	Vah-tseu.°
To perspire.	出汗	Ts'eh °oen.°
To strive.	用力　用心 拚命	Yong° lih; yong° sing; p'ing ming.°
To spill.	打翻	°Tang-fan.
To swim.	游水　弄水	Yeu °sz; long° °sz.
To sing.	唱	Ts'aung.°
To cry.	哭	K'ok.
Don't cry.	勿要哭	'Veh iau° k'ok.
Unable to cry.	哭勿出	K'ok 'veh ts'eh.
To tear.	扯碎	°Ts'a-se.
To wear, to put on (*as clothes*).	著	Tsak.

To put on clothes.	著衣裳	Tsak i-zaung.
To undress.	脫衣裳	T'oeh i-zaung.
To wear a hat, cap or bonnet.	戴帽子	Ta° mau°-°tsz.
To take off the hat.	除帽子	Dzu mau°-°tsz.
To laugh.	笑	Siau°.
Laughable.	好笑	°Hau siau°.
To excite laughter.	惹笑	°Za siau°.
To ridicule.	冷笑	°Lang siau°.
To win (in a race or game).	贏	Yung.
To lose, (do.)	輸	Su.
To kick.	踢	T'ih.
He will kick.	要踢个	Iau° t'ih kuh.
To print.	印	Iung°.
A stamp or chop.	印　印子	Iung°; iung°-°tsz.
To stamp.	打印	°Tang iung°.
Stereotype plates, or blocks.	印板	Iung°-°pan.
To print books.	印書	Iung° su.
To soak through.	印	Iung.°
To leak.	漏	Leu°.
To return what has been borrowed.	還	Wan.
Return it to me.	還拉我　還我	Wan la° °ngoo; wan °ngoo.
Return it to him.	還拉伊	Wan la° yi.
To return in full.	還清爽	Wan ts'ing-°saung.

I have returned it.	還拉哉　還哉	Wan la° tse; wan tse.
Not yet returned.	勿曾還	'Veh-zung wan.
To avenge one'self.	還報　報還	'Wan pau°; pau° wan.
To make good a loss, or expense.	賠還　償還	Be wan; dzaung wan.
Not able to return, or make good.	還勿起	Wan 'veh °chi.
To hoist a sail.	撐篷	Ts'a bong.
To hoist a flag.	撐旗	Ts'a ji.
To lower, or take in a sail.	落篷	Lauh bong.
To anchor.	抛錨	P'au mau.
To take up the anchor.	拔錨	Bah mau.
To pull out, or up.	拔　拔脫	Bah; bah-t'eh.
To pay back by installments.	拔還	Bah-wan.
To draw in, or up by a capstan.	盤	Ben.
To tow, or track (*as a boat*).	捭縴	Pe chien°.
To pull in two.	捭斷	Pe °doen.
To pull down.	捭坍	Pe t'an.
To fall down (*as a house, etc.*)	坍	T'an.
That house will fall.	萬座房子要坍	°Di °zoo raung-°tsz iau° t'an.
To haul (*as on a rope*).	拖	T'oo.
To push; or shove.	攙	Ts'an.
Push him out.	攙出去	Ts'an ts'eh ch'i°.
To step upon.	踏	Dah.

To twist or wring.	捩	Lih.
To press down by a weight; to crush; to oppress.	壓	K'ah.
To squeeze.	刦	Gah.
To beckon.	招	Tsau.
To seize.	拉	'La.
To twist with the fingers.	撚	°'Nyien.
To carry in the arms (*as a child*).	抱	°Bau.
To bow down to; to worship.	拜	Pa.°
To worship idols.	拜佛　拜神道	Pa° veh; pa° zung-dau°.
To take to pieces, or down.	拆	Ts'ak.
Take it down, or to pieces.	拆脫	Ts'ak-t'eh.
To stop.	停　停拉	Ding; ding la°.
To wait.	等	°Tung.
Wait.	等拉	°Tung la.°
Wait a while.	等一歇　等一等	°Tung ih hyih; °tung ih °tung.
Tell him to wait.	叫伊等一等	Kyau° yi °tung ih °tung.
I have no time to wait.	嘸工夫等	M kong-foo °tung.
It will not do to wait.	等勿得	°Tung 'veh tuh.
Wait and see.	等等看	°Tung °tung k'oen°.
How long have you waited?	等之幾時哉	°Tung-tsz °kyi-z tse?

English	Chinese	Romanization
I have waited a long time.	等之長遠哉	°Tung-tsz dzang-°yoen tse.
To put down (a sedan.)	挽平 停轎	°'Wan-bing; ding-jau.
To change.	換 調	Wen°; °diau.
I want you to change your manner.	我要儂換樣式	°Ngoo iau° nong° wen° yang°-suh.
To nail.	釘	Ting°.
To live.	活	Weh.
Living.	活拉	Weh la°.
Lively.	活動	Weh-°dong.
To die.	死	°Si.
He, or it, is dead.	死哉 死脫哉	°Si tse; °si t'eh tse.
All men must die.	人人終要死	Nyung-nyung tsong iau° °si.
To present (as a present).	送	Song°.
To conduct, or accompany, one a short distance.	送	Song°.
To go out and welcome anyone.	迎接	Nyung-tsih.
To stick (in the ground or elsewhere).	插	Ts'ah.
To dye.	染	°Nyien.
To cast down.	擯下來	Gwan° °'au le.
To throw away.	甩脫	Hwah-t'eh.
To meet, to have an interview.	會	We°.
To hold a meeting.	聚會	°Dzui we°.
Did you meet him.	會着否	We°-dzak va°?

I did not; no.	會勿着	Wè° 'veh-dzak.
To call; to tell.	叫 叫	Kyau°; kau.
Call him.	叫伊	Kyau° yi.
Tell him to come.	叫伊來	Kyau° yi le.
To scratch.	抓	°Tsa.
To cut with scissors.	剪	°Tsien.
To pry (*with a lever*).	撬	Ch'au.
To plane.	鉋	Bau°.
To bore.	鑽	Tsoen.
To cut a mortise.	鑿	Zauh.
Ashamed.	坍銃	T'an-ts'ong°.
To varnish; to paint.	漆	Ts'ih.
To weigh.	秤	Ts'ung.
To measure.	量	Liang.
To save; to economise.	省	°Sang.
To save time, or labor.	省工夫	°Sang kong-foo.
To waste; to use extravagantly.	傷	Saung.
To waste time, or labor.	傷工夫	Saung kong-foo.
To use money extravagantly.	傷銅錢	Saung dong-dien.
To seal; to deify; to exalt to a high station.	封	Fong.
Seal it up.	封沒	Fong meh.
To seal up a house.	封門	Fong mung.
To cut; to carve.	切	Ts'ih.
Cut a slice of meat.	切一塊肉	Ts'ih ih kw'e nyok.

Cut a slice of bread.	切一塊饅頭	*Ts'ih ih kw'e° men-deu.*
Cut it open.	切開來	*Ts'ih k'e le.*
To bear upon.	搉	*Chung.°*
Bear upon it.	搉上	*Chung° laung.°*
Press it firmly.	搉住	*Chung°-dzu.*
To loot.	擄　擄物事	*'Loo; 'loo meh-z°.*
To mix; to get things confused.	拌和	*°Ben-°oo°.*
To take by force.	搶　搶物事	*°Ts'iang; °ts'iang meh-z°.*
To deceive; to defraud.	騙拐　拐騙	*P'ien° - °kwa; °kwa-p'ien°.*
A deceiver, a sharper.	拐子	*°Kwa-°tsz.*
To gamble.	賭　賭銅錢	*°Too; °too dong-dien.*
To covet.	貪	*T'en.*
To envy.	妒忌	*°Too-ji°.*
Envious.	妒忌心	*°Too-ji° sing.*
To ascend.	上	*°Zaung.*
Make a record.	上帳	*°Zaung tsang°.*
To ascend a mountain.	上山	*°Zaung san.*
To go up to the capital.	上北京	*°Zaung pok-kyung.*
To go to heaven.	上天	*°Zaung t'ien.*
To land goods.	上貨色	*°Zaung hoo°-suh.*
To oil houses or any wood.	上油	*°Zaung yeu.*
The place of honor.	上首	*°Zaung °seu.*
To put a signature to any instrument of writing.	上名頭	*°Zaung ming-deu.*

To be deceived, or imposed upon.	上當	°Zaung taung°.
To descend.	下	°˙Au.
To descend a mountain.	下山	°˙Au san.
Come down.	下來	°˙Au le.
To go into the country.	下鄉	°˙Au hyang.
To embark.	下船	°˙Au zen.
To ship goods.	下貨色	°˙Au hoo°-suh.
Below.	下底頭	°˙Au °ti-deu.
Underneath.	底下	°Ti-°˙au.
Under the table.	檯底下	De °ti-°˙au.
To desire; to expect; to hope.	望	Maung.°
No hope.	嘸望頭	M maung°-deu.
He has hope.	伊有望頭	Yi °yeu maung°-deu.
To tempt.	引　引誘	°Yung; °yung-yeu°.
To scrape.	括	Kwah.
Scrape it off.	括脫	Kwah-t'eh.
To recognize; to confess.	認	Nyung°.
Do you know me?	認得我否	Nyung°-tuh °ngoo va°?
I don't know you.	我勿認得	°Ngoo 'veh nyung°-tuh.
Does he confess it?	伊認否	Yi nyung° va°?
He won't confess it.	伊勿肯認	Yi 'veh °k'ung nyung°.
To graft; to splice.	接	Tsih.
To tie.	縛	Vok.
Tie it fast.	縛牢	Vok-lau.
To wet; wet.	濕	Sak.

To invite.	請	°Ts'ing.
Invite him in.	請伊進來	°Ts'ing yi tsing° le.
To invite guests.	請客	°Ts'ing k'ak.
Please be seated.	請坐	°Ts'ing-°zoo.
I beg to inquire.	請問	°Ts'ing mung.°
I solicit your instructions.	請教	°Ts'ing kyau.°
To be regretted; placed in an embarrassing position.	難爲情	Nan-we-dzing.
To peck (*as a fowl*).	啄	Zauh.
To lean against.	盈	Ge°.
To repeat from memory.	背	Pe°.
To repeat books.	背書	Pe° su.
To line; or score.	劃	Wak.
To stab.	戳	Ts'ok.
To quarrel.	相罵	Siang-mo°.
To abuse.	罵	Mo°.
To curse.	咒	Tseu°.
To wrangle.	纏	°Dzcn.
To remember.	記	Kyi°.
Memory.	記心	Kyi°-sing.
Bad memory.	記心勿好	Kyi°-sing 'veh °hau.
Remember.	記拉　記得	Kyi°-la°; kyi°-tuh.
To retain; to detain.	留	Lieu.
I will retain one hundred.	我留一百	°Ngoo lieu ih pak.
Could not detain; or retain.	留勿住	Lieu 'veh dzu°.

To sell on credit.	賒	So.
To rely upon.	靠　靠托	K'au°; k'au°-t'auh.
To confide to.	托	T'auh.
You can trust him.	可以靠托	°K'au-°i k'au°-t'auh.
It will not do to trust him.	托勿得	T'auh 'veh tuh.
He is reliable.	托得个	T'auh tuh kuh.
Put not your trust in man.	托勿得人	T'auh 'veh tuh nyung.
To deny; to falsify one's word.	賴	La°.
To ring a bell.	搖鈴	Yau ling.
To row; to shake.	搖　搖船	Yau; yau zen.
To pour out.	倒脫	°Tau-t'eh.
To add to.	加　加點　添　添點	Ka; ka-tien; t'ien; t'ien-tien.
To pile one on top of another.	疊　疊上	Deh; deh laung°.
To pile up.	疊起來	Deh °chi le.
To take from.	拿脫	Nau t'eh.
To take back.	拿轉來	Nau °tsen le.
To calculate.	算	Soen°.
Calculate and see how much.	算算看	Soen°-soen° k'oen°.
I can not calculate.	算勿來	Soen° 'veh le.
An abacus.	算盤	Soen°-ben.
To sleep.	睏	Kw'ung°.
Go to sleep; go lie down.	去睏	Chi° kw'ung°.
He is asleep.	睏起拉	Kw'ung° °chi la°.
Unable to sleep.	睏勿起	Kw'ung° 'veh °chi.

To sleep soundly.	好睏	°Hau kw°ung°.
To sleep late.	睏晚朝	Kw'ung° an° tsau.
He has gone to sleep.	睏起哉	Kw'ung° °chi tse.
To nod; to be drowsy.	瞌銃	K'eh-ts'ong°.
To exchange; to barter.	換 調	Wen°; °diau.
To stir; to agitate.	炒	°Ts'au.
To draw a carriage.	拖馬車	T"oo °mo-ts'o.
To change a dollar into cash.	兌銅錢	De° dong-dien.
To transfer.	劃	Wak.
Transfer it to my name.	劃拉我名下	Wak la° °ngoo ming-°'au.
To pawn.	當 當脫 押 押脫	Taung°; Taung°-t'eh; ah; ah-t'eh.
To hypothecate.	押 押脫	Ah; ah-t'eh.
To whom is it hypothecated?	押拉啥人	Ah la° sa° nyung?
It is hypothecated to me.	押拉我	Ah la° °ngoo.
To secure.	保	°Pau.
A security.	保人	°Pau-nyung.
Will you secure?	儂肯保否	Nong° °k'ung °pau va°?
I am willing to become security.	我肯保个	°Ngoo °k'ung °pau kuh.
I will not secure.	我勿保	°Ngoo 'veh °pau.
To persuade.	勸	Choen°.
To fall sick.	生病	Sang-bing°.
To betroth.	攀親	P'an-ts'ing.
To smell.	嗅	Hong°.

To divide; to separate.	分開	Fung-k'e.
To follow.	跟	Kung.
Follow me.	跟我	Kung °ngoo.
According to; to go towards.	照	Tsau°.
Imitate the sample.	照樣	Tsau° yang°.
Follow my example.	照我	Tsau° °ngoo.
To solder.	銲	'Oen°.
To cast; to found.	澆　鑄	Kyau; tsu°.
To cast a cannon.	鑄砲	Tsu° p'au°.
To melt; to dissolve.	烊	Yang.
To freeze.	冰膠	Ping-kau.
To congeal; to coagulate.	結　結攏	Kyih; kyih-°long.
To turn (as a wheel).	轉	°Tsen.
To float.	氽	°T'ung.
To fail in business.	倒賬	°Tau tsang°.
To prop.	撐	Ts'ang.
To save.	救	Kyeu°.
Save me.	救救我	Kyeu°-kyeu° °ngoo.
To pray.	求　禱告	Jeu; °Tau-kau°.
To repent.	悔改	Hwe°-°ke.
To regret.	懊憹	°Au-lau°.
To guard against; to be watchful.	防備	Baung-be°.
To care for; be careful.	當心　小心	Taung-sing; °Siau-sing.
To quarrel (as husband and wife).	淘氣	Dau-chi°.

To punish.	罰辦	Vah-ban°.
To reduce; to take from.	齾	Ngah.
I will cut your wages.	我要齾儂工錢	°Ngoo iau° ngah nong° kong-dien.
To translate.	繙　繙譯	Fan; fan-yuh.
To interpret.	繙話　傳話	Fan-wo°; dzen-wo°.
To manage; to have the management.	經手	Kyung-°seu.
To turn round.	旋轉來	Zien°-°tsen le.
To turn over.	翻轉來	Fan °tsen le.
To consult.	商量　斟酌	Saung-liang; tsung-tsak.
To run (*as water*).	流	Lieu.
To skin; to peel; to strip.	剝	Pok.
To feel; to touch.	摸	Mok.
To guess.	猜猜	Ts'oe-ts'oe.
Guess.	猜猜看	Ts'oe-ts'oe k'oen°.
To examine; to scrutinize.	查	Dzo.
Examine.	查查看	Dzo-dzo k'oen°.
Unable to find out by examination.	查勿出	Dzo 'veh ts'eh.
To prove; to evince.	對　對證	Te°; te°-tsung°.
To play (*as an instrument with the fingers*).	彈	Dan.
To reject.	退　退脫	T'e°; t'e°-t'eh.
To sport; to frolic; to trifle.	字相　弄字相	Beh-siang°; long°-beh-siang°.
To yield; to give place.	讓	Nyang°.

To soak; to immerse; to baptize.	浸	Tsiny°.
To gain (*profit*). To make money.	賺	°Dzan.
Profit.	賺頭	°Dzan-deu.
To lose, etc.	蝕　蝕脫　蝕本	Zeh; zeh-t'eh; zeh-°pung.
To become rich.	發財	Fah-dze.
To heal.	醫好　看好	I-°hau; k'oen°-°hau.
To spread; to propagate (*as disease or a report*).	發　發開	Fah; fah-k'e.
To jump; to leap.	跳	T'iau°.
To climb.	爬	Bo.
To crawl.	邉	Ban.
To splash.	蹩　蹩起來　蹩開	Zan°; zan° °chi le; zan°-k'e.
To boil (*as water*).	滾	°Kwung.
To nurse (*the sick*).	須帳	Su-tsang°.
To sit or stay with for company.	倍	Be°.
To slander.	話瘵	Wo°-°liau.
To lock; a lock.	鎖	°Soo.
To bolt; a bolt or bar.	閂	Sak.
To roll.	滾	°Kwung.
To string (*as cash*).	穿	Ts'en.
To comfort.	安慰	Oen-'we°.
To injure.	害	'E°.
To degrade.	革　革脫	Kak; kak-t'eh.
To burn (*as fuel*).	燒	Sau.

To gather (*as fruit or flowers*).	採	°Ts‘e.
To cancel; to erase.	圈脫	Choen-t‘eh.
To reconcile; to pacify.	和　勸和	‘Oo; choen°-‘oo.
To pay a balance.	找　找還	°Tsau; °tsau-wan.
To criticise.	批評	P‘i-bing.
To answer.	回頭	We-deu.
To cook.	燒　燒飯	Sau; sau van°.
To send forth; to issue.	出	Ts‘eh.
To issue a proclamation.	出告示	Ts‘eh kau°-z°.
To violate (*a regulation or law*).	犯　犯法	°Van; °van fah.
To drive; to urge; to press.	趕	°Koen.
To grind; to whet.	磨	Moo.
To plaster (*as a wall*).	粉　粉壁	°Fung; °fung-pih.
To file.	剉	Ts‘oo°.
To pound (*in a mortar*).	舂	Song (ts‘ung°).
To sift.	篩	Sz (sa).
To strain; to filter.	瀝	Lih.
To water (*a garden*).	澆	Kyau.
To separate; to make distinct.	理　理清爽	°Li; °li ts‘ing-°saung.
To create a disturbance.	作反	Tsauh-°fan.
To hinder; to frustrate.	阻　阻擋	°Tsoo; °tsoo-°taung.
To separate; to divide.	分開　分別	Fung-k‘e; fung-pih.
Recommend (*for a position*).	薦	Tsien°.

To encroach upon (another's land).	佔	Tsien°.
To take up with both hands.	掇	Toeh.
To uncover; to open.	揭　揭開	Hyih; hyih-k'e.
To point with the hand.	點　指點	°Tien, °tsz-°tien.
To stultify.	膽倒	Dung-°tau.
To vacillate; to disappoint.	搭橋	Tah-jau.
To deport one's self to; to treat.	待	°De.
I treated him kindly.	我待伊蠻好	°Ngoo °de yi 'man °hau.
To offend; to transgress.	得罪	Tuh-°dzoe.
To hide or secrete one's self.	叛攏	Ben°-°long.
To consult.	商量	Saung-liang.
To consider.	打算	°Tang-soen°.
To spread, daub, or smear.	搨	T'ah.
To arrange, to manage.	辦	Ban°.
To kneel.	跪	°Jui.
To banish.	充軍	Ts'ong-kyuin.
To forfeit.	失脫	Seh-t'eh.
To confiscate.	充公　入官	Ts'ong-kong; zeh-kwen.
To rebel.	逆	Nyuh.
To forbid; to prohibit.	勿許	'Veh-°hyui.
To make a prostration (as before an idol).	磕頭	K'eh-deu.
To add to.	加	Ka.

Add a little.	加點	*Ka-tien.*
To hook.	鉤	*Keu.*
To deceive, to mystify.	迷惑	*Mi-'ok.*
To deceive, to trick.	弄成	*Long°-dzung.*
To sacrifice to.	祭	*Tsi°.*
Finished.	完哉	*Wen-tse.*

www.ingramcontent.com/pod-product-compliance
Lightning Source LLC
Chambersburg PA
CBHW030243170426
43202CB00009B/610